T0265618

Praise for *Don't Look Back*

"In recent years on my hardest days, all I wanted to do was to crawl back into bed and not have to face the new realities that were in front of me. My life looked very different than I thought it would, and I desperately needed some time to adjust to all the changes. In *Don't Look Back*, Christine guides those of us who may be feeling stuck in pain and in the past yet are wanting to thrive while moving forward into a hopeful future. This is a book to sit with yourself, and to share with your loved ones who also need this timely encouragement!"

—LYSA TERKEURST, #1 *NEW YORK TIMES* BESTSELLING
AUTHOR AND PRESIDENT OF PROVERBS 31 MINISTRIES

"My friend, Christine Caine's latest book is a masterclass on the power of perspective. In *Don't Look Back*, she reminds us to keep our eyes fixed on what's most important—God's plan for our lives. We may not always know where he's leading us, but we can keep moving forward in faith knowing that he's prepared the way."

—STEVEN FURTICK, LEAD PASTOR OF ELEVATION CHURCH
AND *NEW YORK TIMES* BESTSELLING AUTHOR OF *CRASH
THE CHATTERBOX*, *GREATER*, AND *(UN)QUALIFIED*

"*Don't Look Back* is bursting with the one thing everyone is in desperate need of these days: *hope*. Hope for the future because of the abiding hope found only in Jesus. There is no greater voice to speak to this than Christine's. She is a prophet to our generation and I'm certain this book will change your life!"

—CARLOS WHITTAKER, SPEAKER, STORYTELLER,
AND AUTHOR OF *HOW TO HUMAN*

"Several research studies have concluded that we spend as much as 30 percent of our mental capacity thinking about the past. Even more troubling, when we think about the past, the majority of our thoughts gravitate to our regrets. In *Don't Look Back*, Christine Caine delivers a powerful toolbox to help shift our thoughts in the direction God has always called us to focus: heavenward. This book is the counselor we all need on speed dial."

—NONA JONES, PREACHER, TECH EXECUTIVE,
AND AUTHOR OF *KILLING COMPARISON*

"Most of us feel stuck at some point in our lives. We want to change, but we don't know how. Thankfully, Christine Caine has written *Don't Look Back*. Packed with spiritual wisdom and practical application, this book will equip and inspire you to take real steps of faith and live the life God intended for you."

—CRAIG GROESCHEL, FOUNDING PASTOR OF LIFE.CHURCH
AND *NEW YORK TIMES* BESTSELLING AUTHOR

"When you meet Chris—and you will meet her in this book—you will discover a woman that could have stayed stuck by looking back at her pain, disadvantages, and trauma. But instead of looking back, she's looking to Jesus. Jesus will never leave you stuck. Get this book. Devour it. Share it. Live it."

—DR. DERWIN L. GRAY, COFOUNDER AND LEAD PASTOR OF
TRANSFORMATION CHURCH AND AUTHOR OF *THE GOOD LIFE*

"At some point in life, you may find yourself stuck, and you'll be tempted to stay where you are or to return to what was. With her signature prophetic voice, Christine Caine calls us to move forward in obedience to Jesus. There is no way to grow without stepping out in faith. Her message is personal to me: Chris was a significant voice in my own life during a key season of discerning a call to step out with faith and courage. As she unpacks the Scripture and shares stories from her life and from others around the world, I know you will find the strength, healing, and hope to live with greater purpose and freedom."

—GLENN PACKIAM, LEAD PASTOR AT ROCKHARBOR CHURCH AND
AUTHOR OF *THE RESILIENT PASTOR* AND *THE INTENTIONAL YEAR*

DON'T LOOK
BACK

ALSO BY CHRISTINE CAINE

To my beloved daughters, Catherine and Sophia

"Remember Lot's wife!"

JESUS, LUKE 17:32

Contents

CONTENTS

INTRODUCTION

Where You Look Is
Where You Will Go

M rs. Caine! Keep your eyes straight ahead. Let your peripheral vision do the work. Use your mirrors. Remember that where you look, you will go! I don't want to see your head on a swivel. I don't want to see you looking back. Eyes forward!"

My motorcycle safety course instructor belted out most everything he had been teaching me as I exited the last turn and came to a stop. Feeling a bit proud of myself for having mastered the obstacle course he'd designed with orange cones, it must have shown on my face, because before I could look around to accept any fist bumps from my fellow riders, he added, "But don't let me see you on the interstate with that toy, even if it is legal."

With that, everyone laughed, much like they had the past

two days. Ever since I rolled up to the California Motorcyclist Safety Course on my Vespa—wearing my riding gear, complete with elbow and knee pads, boots, and a helmet that made me look like a bobblehead—and took my place among all the other riders, they had simply stared at me in disbelief. I felt welcomed enough among the mostly twenty-something-year-olds straddling their sport bikes, but it was hard to ignore that I was obviously the oldest in the class and the only married-mum-with-kids type.

As I mastered each exercise, little by little I garnered their respect—well, as much respect as you can get on what most people classify as a scooter or a moped. I imagine if I had been on a Ducati, I would have had immediate respect, but showing up on a pretty little Vespa meant I had to earn it. Or at least be a good sport and laugh at myself as much as they all did.

It was the fall of 2020, when things were starting to open up a bit after being shut down during the pandemic. The state of California resumed their Motorcyclist Safety Course because it could be held outdoors and met the requirements for social distancing. And since I wasn't traveling as much because of COVID-19 restrictions, I had a little more time available in my schedule. So I finally booked the course I had been trying to fit in for years.

What made it feel even more important to me is that my husband, Nick, had surprised me for my fiftieth birthday with the Vespa—something I had enjoyed immensely when we lived in Australia. There I owned a hot-pink one, and I rode

DON'T LOOK
BACK

GETTING UNSTUCK AND MOVING
FORWARD WITH PASSION AND PURPOSE

CHRISTINE CAINE

NELSON
BOOKS

An Imprint of Thomas Nelson

Published in Nashville, Tennessee, by Nelson Books, an imprint of Thomas Nelson. Nelson Books and Thomas Nelson are registered trademarks of HarperCollins Christian Publishing, Inc.

Published in association with Yates & Yates, www.yates2.com.

Thomas Nelson titles may be purchased in bulk for educational, business, fundraising, or sales promotional use. For information, please email SpecialMarkets@ThomasNelson.com.

Unless otherwise noted, scripture quotations are taken from the Christian Standard Bible®, Copyright © 2017 by Holman Bible Publishers. Used by permission. Christian Standard Bible® and CSB® are federally registered trademarks of Holman Bible Publishers.

Scripture quotations marked AMP are taken from the Amplified® Bible (AMP). Copyright © 2015 by The Lockman Foundation. Used by permission. www.lockman.org.

Scripture quotations marked BLB are taken from The Holy Bible, Berean Literary Bible. Copyright ©2016, 2020 by Bible Hub. Used by Permission. All Rights Reserved Worldwide. https://literalbible.com/.

Scripture quotations marked ESV are taken from the ESV® Bible (The Holy Bible, English Standard Version®). Copyright © 2001 by Crossway, a publishing ministry of Good News Publishers. Used by permission. All rights reserved.

Scripture quotations marked GNT are taken from the Good News Translation in Today's English Version—Second Edition. Copyright © 1992 by American Bible Society. Used by permission.

Scripture quotations marked MSG are taken from The Message. Copyright © 1993, 2002, 2018 by Eugene H. Peterson. Used by permission of NavPress. All rights reserved. Represented by Tyndale House Publishers, a Division of Tyndale House Ministries.

Scripture quotations marked NIV are taken from The Holy Bible, New International Version®, NIV®. Copyright © 1973, 1978, 1984, 2011 by Biblica, Inc.® Used by permission of Zondervan. All rights reserved worldwide. www.Zondervan.com. The "NIV" and "New International Version" are trademarks registered in the United States Patent and Trademark Office by Biblica, Inc.®

Scripture quotations marked NLT are taken from the Holy Bible, New Living Translation. Copyright © 1996, 2004, 2015 by Tyndale House Foundation. Used by permission of Tyndale House Publishers, Inc., Carol Stream, Illinois 60188. All rights reserved.

Any internet addresses, phone numbers, or company or product information printed in this book are offered as a resource and are not intended in any way to be or to imply an endorsement by Thomas Nelson, nor does Thomas Nelson vouch for the existence, content, or services of these sites, phone numbers, companies, or products beyond the life of this book.

Some names and identifying factors have been changed to protect the privacy of those who have shared their stories.

ISBN 978-1-4002-2657-3 (HC)
ISBN 978-1-4002-2664-1 (eBook)
ISBN 978-1-4002-3146-1 (IE)

Library of Congress Cataloging-in-Publication Data on File

Printed in the United States of America

24 25 26 27 28 LBC 10 9 8 7 6

it everywhere. But when we got ready to move to the United States, it wasn't practical to ship, so I left it behind—but I never stopped pining for it.

In the process of purchasing the Vespa, Nick had researched everything for me, and he informed me that in order to enjoy my new bike beyond the end of the driveway, I had to take an instructional riding course and pass a written exam. As much as I wanted to just trade in my Australian motorcycle license for a California one, that wasn't going to work. So I studied in advance and passed the written exam with flying colors. However, the riding course was a little more challenging—especially since the last time I'd ridden a bike for any significant amount of time, I'd been driving on the other side of the road. Still, getting my motorcycle license was imperative if I wanted to be free to ride anywhere in the US.

WHERE YOU LOOK, YOU WILL GO

Of all that I learned during the motorcycle safety course, one phrase my instructor used repeatedly never left me: *Where you look, you will go.* For weeks after the course, it resounded in my head. And because the pandemic was ongoing, I especially thought about it in relationship to my pre- and post-pandemic life. I recognized that my natural inclination was to compare life before the pandemic to life after the pandemic. To look back, rather than forward. To find myself expressing frustration and saying to no one in particular, "When will we go back to normal?"

Maybe you said the same thing. When the pandemic hit us all and stretched around the globe in 2020, and well into 2021, how could we not want to roll back the clock, return to the way it used to be, and do things the way we had always done them?

What changed in those days? Far more than had stayed the same. In my pre-pandemic life, my kids could be dropped off at school. Nick and I could go to an office to work. I could meet face-to-face with my team. I could travel freely. It was hard learning new ways of communicating via Zoom, of speaking to a camera instead of visiting churches, of fighting human trafficking with all the new restrictions.

It was then I recognized that where I looked, I would go. Where my mind went, I would go. Where my emotions went, I would go. I had to remember my purpose and calling. How I did things had to change, no doubt, but I also needed to remember that the promises and purposes of God had not changed at all.

All of it got me to thinking—there are times in each of our lives when we look back and feel desperate to make time stand still, particularly when change happens that we didn't see coming. Isn't that what Lot's wife did when God sent the angels to escort her and her family out of Sodom? She looked back and turned into a pillar of salt.[1] I can't wait to introduce you to her in chapter 1, because what I've learned from her and from my own experiences is that we can't stop and look back any more than she did. Looking back didn't go well for her, and it never goes well for us either. What's more, looking back doesn't enable us to *go* back, and more times than not, it just makes us *stuck*. In a place. In a space. In a memory. In a habit. In a mindset. When we are stuck, we are not moving ahead because we can't move ahead when our feet are planted in place.

When Jesus invites us into a relationship with him, it is an invitation to follow him.[2] When we accept his invitation, we don't know where we are going, how long it will take us, or what we will encounter along the way—but what we do know is that he will never leave us nor forsake us.[3] Following Jesus is a journey, moving from one place to another, not necessarily geographically but always spiritually. Furthermore, to follow Jesus, we have to go where he is leading, and as much as we might want, we can't spend all our time looking back to where we once were while simultaneously trying to look forward to where he is taking us. In the words of King Solomon, "Let your eyes look straight ahead; fix your gaze directly before you."[4]

Life is full of unexpected twists and turns, of detours and slowdowns, of surprising stops that divert our focus. In recent years, we've had a lot of them no matter where we live around the globe. We've navigated life through a pandemic and all the loss that goes with it. So many of us lost loved ones and dear friends, relationships and jobs, ministries and businesses, hopes and dreams. It's still hard to comprehend. On top of that, more happened around the world in that time than we could have ever imagined—politically, economically, environmentally, and socially.

I think we'd all agree that it's shocking how we can be moving forward, full steam ahead, and suddenly life throws something our way that changes everything, whether it affects everyone in the world or just us. If we've not prepared ourselves for how to move through those times, and get our vision looking ahead once more, we can get stuck looking back. We can get stuck in places we never intended to find ourselves—spiritually, emotionally, mentally, relationally, financially, or physically. To be honest, we can get stuck just about anywhere in life, can't we?

- When we like where we are.
- When we are scared about the future.
- When we may not want to let go of what we love.
- When we are wronged.
- When we are hurt.
- When we are disappointed.
- When we are numb from the trauma we've endured.
- When we are betrayed.
- When we are weary.
- When we are overwhelmed.
- When we are discouraged.
- When we are distracted.
- When we are wounded.
- When we are hopeless.

Sometimes, when we stop and think about what we have experienced, how can we not get stuck in disappointment, unforgiveness, bitterness, offense, fear, guilt, anxiety, insecurity, indifference, apathy, comfort, or complacency? And yet, to move forward, we have to find a way to move through these exact places and more. We have to move through loss, grief, hardship, suffering, disillusionment, mistakes, and sheer heartache to keep going.

Still, I imagine we all find it easier to stay stuck than risk moving forward and what might come with it, like stepping out into unfamiliar terrain and feeling even more uncomfortable. Like experiencing more hurt, more disappointment, more suffering, or more betrayal. It's little wonder the writer of Hebrews said that we must focus our eyes on Jesus. "Fixing our eyes on Jesus, the pioneer and perfecter of faith. For the joy set before him he endured the cross, scorning its shame, and sat down at the right hand of the throne of God."[5]

To keep going through the most painful part of his mission, Jesus kept his focus on the joy that lay before him. That's how he endured the cross and made it to his seat at the right hand of God the Father in heaven. Because of Christ's sacrifice, we won't ever have to go through the kind of suffering he did—but we will still go through our own times of pain and hardship, of disappointment and hurt, of loss and heartache. Keeping our eyes on Jesus, who is the way, is the only way we can find our way forward.

Successfully navigating the twists and turns of life while

fixing our eyes on Jesus requires a spiritual strategy with four steps:

1. We need to first learn how to stop looking back and start looking to Jesus.
2. We need to invite Jesus in to help us get unstuck from those places where we never meant to be.
3. We need to start moving forward in a way that ensures we're successfully pursuing all the plans, purposes, and promises God has for our lives.
4. What's more, we need to learn how to do this repeatedly in every area of our lives all throughout our lives, because new challenges will present themselves—Jesus told us they would. He said we would have trouble in this world, but he also told us how to move through what life would throw our way.[6]

I understand how challenging this can be, particularly because it is not something we do once and move on. As we journey together through the pages of this book, I pray you will discover how to stop looking back and start looking to Jesus, how to move on from where you are to where God wants you to be, how to look forward to the future God has for you, and how to keep moving toward it in bold faith—especially when the world is ever-changing.

Love, Chris

PART ONE

Why Moving Forward Is Important

ONE

The World Is Always Changing, God Remains the Same

Lord . . . we are grateful for your protection and provision, and for everything that you have already done, and everything you have prepared for us ahead. We trust you . . . we know you have so much for us as an organization here in Ukraine and globally . . . we are so grateful that we are able to be your hands and your feet to rescue people . . . that we can help people have freedom and restoration . . . keep our hearts that we would notice and see the miracles that you're doing around us. Thank you, Lord.

JULIA, A21 COUNTRY MANAGER, UKRAINE, SAFE
HOUSE OUTSIDE KYIV, FEBRUARY 11, 2022

Clutching my chest, swallowing hard, it was all I could do to voice my *amen*. Never in all the years of A21 had I witnessed such courage, such strength, such faith in our team. Julia and two of our Ukraine team—Liliia and Yuliia—had joined our global team meeting from a safe house outside Kyiv. They had been there for a couple of days, along with their husbands and children. Nadiia, another team member, joined from another location inside Ukraine. There were more than one hundred and fifty of our A21 team members from sixteen countries gathered in what we affectionately called the upper Zoom room. Since the pandemic had started in 2020, and we all began to work from home, Zoom calls were where we met to connect and update each other on the work of A21 and our other ministries from around the world. Today, we were linked together in prayer over something none of our offices had ever faced—the threat of a war in a city where we had an A21 office.

Finding my voice, I shouted to Julia and the rest of the team huddled together on a sofa, "We're here for you and are with you all the way. Whatever you need, we are here to help. We love you! Stay safe!"

As everyone else waved bye and began disappearing from my screen, I held on. For as long as I could. Never had I felt so responsible for so many. Never had I felt so desperate for them to be out of harm's way. Never had I wanted to be on the other side of the world more. And as my tears spilled, so did my prayers. How could I not cry my prayers? *Lord, please be their refuge and their fortress. Cover them under your wings. Protect them from any harm. Have mercy on everyone in Ukraine.*

Making my way to the garage, I found Nick still staring

at his computer screen, though everyone was gone from the meeting. It weighed just as heavily on him as it did me. Letting the silence hold us, he didn't move. He didn't say a word. Truth be told, he didn't need to. It had all been said. For days we'd been talking. To each other. To Julia. To our A21 chief operations officer, Phil. To our security team, Tony and Andreas. To our contacts in Washington, DC, and Europe. To all our other country managers around the globe. To the pastors of our three Zoe churches in Warsaw, Thessaloniki, and Sofia. After all, it was clear they would all be involved in helping anyone fleeing Ukraine, being the hands and feet of Jesus, as Julia so beautifully prayed. Whatever move Russia made, we were prepared—as prepared as one can be for an impending war.

WHEN RUSSIA INVADED UKRAINE

After what felt like an unusually long day, perhaps because of all the updates coming out of Ukraine and calls back and forth with our team, Nick and I turned in for the night. We'd barely fallen asleep when Nick's phone rang. It was Andreas, and in the quiet of the night, I could hear every word. Russia had begun launching missiles and invading Ukraine. Julia and the team would have to move quickly. It was 5:30 a.m. at the safe house. He would give them time to get the kids up, eat breakfast, and pack, but that was all. Counterattack missiles were already flying over their heads. There was nothing to do but move forward. There was no going back to Kyiv.

Nick had brought Tony and Andreas onto our team to expand security for all our A21 offices. After a trafficker threatened members of our European team in court, it was clear that we needed to do more to ensure everyone on our team was protected. But never did we expect the need to include a plan to escape an invasion.

For a long while after the call, Nick and I lay awake in the dark. I couldn't help but pray for each person staying in the safe house, putting before the Lord what I felt each of them needed, especially Julia's husband, Slava. In the weeks leading up to the invasion, each night after they had tucked their two boys in bed, Julia said they would talk about what might happen if a war started and what they would do. She said it wasn't easy to hear what was in his heart, but she understood. He wanted to stay and help and do what he was called to do. As the care pastor for their church, he wanted to stay and care for the people of Kyiv, to prepare the church building to serve as a refuge, shelter, hospital, or place to distribute meals—whatever the people of Kyiv would need it to be. He was Ukrainian. They both were. And together, they were followers of Christ who had committed to a life of faith, a life of serving, a life of caring for others. Of course he would stay, and she would go. For the sake of the boys, for the sake of her team, for the sake of every potential victim of human trafficking. From her work at A21, Julia knew that the most vulnerable to trafficking during a war are women and children. She knew she could do more to help prevent trafficking and reach the vulnerable if she were based in Poland, if she could work on the border helping the multitudes who would inevitably be fleeing Ukraine in search of safety.

When morning came, neither Nick nor I had slept as much as we had prayed. When Andreas updated us, he said the team was on the road, but he and Tony were changing their route, and most likely, they would keep changing it, even if it meant passing up safe houses they had secured and hoped to use. It appeared best to press on to Julia's relative's home in western Ukraine.

WORTH THE TRIP

A month earlier, I had flown to Europe to visit some of our European offices and team. After not being able to travel outside the United States for two long years due to COVID-19 travel restrictions, I was determined to be in the same room with as many of our team as I could. I wanted to see their faces and look into their eyes, without a computer screen separating us. I decided before I traveled that I was not going to compare it to pre-COVID travel life. I chose to adjust my mindset in advance. Nothing would ever be like it once was, so what was the point of looking back?

It was a hard trip. Because of the omicron variant. Because

of all the paperwork required by each country. Because of all the restrictions. Because of all the COVID-19 tests. Never had I taken so many. But it was all so worth it. Seeing our teams, sharing meals, talking until the wee hours of the morning, hearing even more about all the creative ways they'd found to keep in touch with survivors during lockdowns—it seemed more like an awesome reunion. We were so happy to actually see each other.

I'll never forget being in Warsaw, eager to travel on to Kyiv next to see Julia and the team there, when Andreas called Nick. It was already too dangerous for us to travel to Kyiv, he said, and if we got there, it was possible we wouldn't be able to get out. The Russians had surrounded Ukraine on three sides. From all indications, it was just a matter of time before the invasion started.

From my perspective, if it wasn't safe enough for us to travel to Ukraine, then it wasn't safe enough for our team to stay. Nick agreed. We both wanted them relocated to Warsaw as quickly as possible. From what Andreas said, Julia was almost ready. She and the team had reached a safe house outside Kyiv but were still making trips back to the city for supplies.

The morning Andreas called Julia to say it was time to go, though she'd been preparing for weeks, deep down she still wasn't ready. She had hoped for more time with her husband, Slava. That's where her heart weighed most heavily. How could it not? When would she see him again? Would they be the same? What was all this going to do to their boys? And yet, she knew the team had to go. She knew it was best. For her. For Liliia and Yuliia. For their husbands. For their girls and their boys. If they had to run for their lives, then they would do it for the sake of the next generation.

RUNNING FOR THEIR LIVES

I've never had to run for my life, though my grandparents did, and then a generation later, my parents did. My grandparents fled Izmir, Turkey, for Greece, and then to Egypt, in 1922, during the Greek Genocide. There, in Alexandria, Egypt, a truly cosmopolitan city and the gateway to Europe, they worked to reestablish their lives and raise their family in peace. But in 1952, the nationalist generals overthrew King Farouk and became a powerful force. Christians became a persecuted minority, and both my parents, who were young and single and didn't know each other, fled from Egypt. My mother was just sixteen when her parents put her and her sister on a ship to Australia. If they couldn't save the whole family, then they would save their children. With tens of thousands of other Greek families,[1] my mother and her sister landed in Australia with next to nothing. Somehow, they each managed to work two jobs, saving enough money to buy passage for their parents and brother to make the same journey they did. Like my mum and her sister, they came with one suitcase each, leaving everything else behind.

When I was growing up, Mum never spoke of any of this. Neither did my aunt or my uncle. It was something I later learned they would all rather leave in the past. To this day, it is unimaginable to me the fear Mum must have faced and the courage she surely mustered. I can only guess at the weight of responsibility she carried for her sister and brother, for her mum and dad.

When she later met my dad in Sydney, they fell in love and married. From what I observed growing up, whatever they both experienced fleeing from Egypt, they didn't spend time looking back. Together, they forged a new life and, with the rest of our extended family, made Australia home.

A CLOUD BY DAY AND A PILLAR BY NIGHT

For four days, Andreas and Tony kept Julia and the team moving forward from a distance. They called her every hour. They reassured her they were watching her every move. In three cars, the entire team and their families caravanned across the country. In small towns, they refueled. Andreas had given them a list of supplies to pack, including extra fuel, but as long as stations had fuel, they would purchase what they needed. The jugs of fuel would be for when the stations ran out. In one town, the line for fuel was more than one hundred cars, and each car was allowed a ration of only twenty-one liters.

Never once did they stop. Instead, they took turns driving

so each of them could nap and they could keep going. From satellite images, Andreas watched from his office in Europe all night, every night, and Tony watched from his office in the US all day, every day. When a fellow A21 team member, Mi Yung, sent Julia a text reminding her of God's protection over the children of Israel when they escaped Egypt, she recounted how God led Moses and the children of Israel with a cloud by day and a pillar by night.[2] To Julia, Andreas and Tony were just like the cloud and the pillar. It meant everything to know that someone was watching over them. To know they were not alone.

One evening, as they waited in line for fuel, a man came walking along the line of cars with a teapot. He was offering hot water for people to make coffee or tea. Later that night, he came back, only this time he brought his wife. She had made a pot of borscht and wanted everyone in their cars to eat. They all agreed it was the best borscht they had ever eaten. She'd even boiled eggs for them to save for later.

When they finally walked in the door of Julia's relatives' home, in the western part of Ukraine, seeing the table set with an abundance of food suddenly felt so normal. Watching her boys hug her family brought a kind of relief she hadn't felt in days. She could feel her anxiety give way to hope, her fear give way to renewed courage. Taking it all in felt like a gentle reminder that God was with them, watching over them, and going before them, even while the world as they knew it was crumbling behind them.

YOU CAN'T STAY

When Andreas called Julia the next time, it was much sooner than the hour mark. "Julia, I know you've just arrived, and I know you're relieved to see your family," he said, "but you can't stay. I can give you an hour and a half to eat, rest, and enjoy your relatives, and then you have to head for the border tonight."

Crossing the border into Poland was more of a contingency plan than a predetermined one. But from the beginning, the team was prepared that if the invasion escalated, that's where they would go. Though Julia held out hope they could all stay inside the borders of their home country, during the time they'd been on the road, the bombing of the capital city had intensified, as did the shelling all across the country.

When Andreas told her that the men could be restricted from crossing the border with the women and children, she had to steel herself before passing on such news. Martial law had been declared and a government regulation prohibited all men between the ages of eighteen and sixty from leaving the country.[3]

For the next two and a half days, Julia and the team inched along in a line that was miles long and led to a border crossing. With no bathrooms, no showers, and nothing for the kids to do, they did their best to hide their fear and keep their kids busy. The dirt on the cars became whiteboards on which the kids drew with their fingers. Grassy fields alongside the road turned into playgrounds. Mealtimes turned into picnics. Watching as others ran out of fuel, abandoned their cars, and began walking, often carrying children and pulling suitcases, they couldn't help but agonize over whether they'd actually make it. In one of his last calls to Julia, Andreas prepared her for what lay ahead.

Szymon, our Zoe Warsaw pastor, was at the border waiting for her. He'd been there for two days. It was certain that the men would not be allowed to cross, but Tony was working on a plan for where they could go to be safe. They would need to rearrange the contents of the cars, leaving any remaining supplies in one car for the men to take. And their goodbyes would need to be quick.

I can't tell you the relief we all felt when our group crossed the border—and the millions more who came after them.

WHAT NEXT?

When the war in Ukraine started, it seemed like a continuation of all that had been happening for the past couple of years. After all, starting in 2020, in addition to moving through a global pandemic, we had experienced natural disasters on most every continent—hurricanes, wildfires, tornadoes, drought, and flooding.[4] The ground warmed enough in the mid-Atlantic region for billions of cicadas to emerge—after seventeen years of being underground.[5] It was reminiscent of a plague of biblical proportions. We saw protests and riots in major cities in more than sixty countries, drawing attention to racial injustice.[6] It was easy to understand why some people wanted to throw their hands up in the air and ask, "What's next?"—because it did feel like one thing after another just kept happening. When people questioned whether it was the end of the world, it was—even though we're all still here—because it was the end of the world as we once knew it.

Like most everyone, I was tempted to look back. To want to go back. To 2019. Or any year of our lives before 2020. To go back to normal, whatever our normal was. To forget the new normal that we were all desperately trying to create. Yet, no matter how much I longed to go back to normal, there was no going back. That world as we knew it was finished, and God was beckoning me, along with everyone else, to move forward, to lay hold of his purpose and promises in the future.

Sorting through the tension of not looking back and trying to move forward—including trying to figure out how to move at all in a locked-down world—I began reminding myself that while the world had changed, God had not. He was the same as he'd always been, and I could depend on him to guide me forward.[7]

During that same season of doing my best not to look back and instead to keep moving forward, I was reminded of a woman in the Bible who looked back when she wasn't supposed to, and it didn't go well for her. I mentioned her earlier in the introduction as Lot's wife. She was the woman

running for her life with her
family in Genesis 19. As they ran,
destruction was raining down on
their hometown of Sodom, and
despite being told by an angel
not to look back, she turned and
looked back. Scripture tells us,
"But Lot's wife looked back and
became a pillar of salt."[8]

> I began reminding myself that while the world had changed, God had not.

What makes Lot's wife especially significant is that Jesus said for us to remember her. In the middle of an eschatological discourse in the New Testament, Jesus dropped in three words: "Remember Lot's wife."[9]

If you've ever read Luke 17, it's all too easy to miss these three words. I know because I did for years. I read them, of course, but that's all. I flew past them. But Jesus never wastes a word, let alone three, so there must be some significance in this second-shortest verse in the Bible. (If you didn't know that fun fact, now you do. Perhaps it will help you win your next Bible quiz.) These three words began to show me the importance of not looking back. Of always moving forward. Even in the midst of a pandemic or a war or something far more normal. They became words I couldn't forget and words that showed me the way forward.

Remember Lot's wife.

For thirty-plus years now, I've been going to women's conferences, and I don't remember ever hearing a message on Lot's wife, nor do I remember teaching one. And yet, of the possible 170 women mentioned in Scripture,[10] she is the only one that Jesus tells us to remember. Why her? Why not Eve, Sarah, Miriam, Deborah, Ruth, Rahab, Esther, Elizabeth, or even Mary, his own mother? Of all the women Jesus could have told us to remember, he mentioned only one: Lot's wife. (For all the Bible scholars reading this, Jesus did tell us that the *deed* of the woman who poured oil over him would be remembered forever,[11] but he told us to remember only one woman—Lot's wife.) This is astonishing to me. Why her? There had to be a reason.

LONGINGLY SHE LINGERED

Lot's wife gets one cameo in the Old Testament and one in the New Testament. That's it. That's all Scripture records. Why would Jesus tell us to remember a woman who appears on the pages of Scripture only long enough to disappear? A woman who has the shortest bio ever. A woman whose proper name we don't even know. What is it about her that we're to remember?

As I began to study her life, I noted something very important. This woman was told one thing: "Don't look back." And the one thing she was told not to do is the one thing she did. Furthermore, I found that understanding *how* she looked back quite possibly held a clue as to *why* she looked back: "But Lot's wife, from behind him, [foolishly, longingly] looked [back toward Sodom in an act of disobedience], and she became a pillar of salt."[12]

She looked back longingly in an act of disobedience. I don't want to be harsh about Lot's wife. We all make mistakes, and we all disobey, and to think she looked back longingly causes me to feel for her. Here she was, living her life as usual, and suddenly she's told to pack up and run for her life. All the while an angel is holding her hand and guiding her.

Even reading her story afresh while writing, compassion overtook me. I couldn't help but think of Julia fleeing Ukraine. I thought of my grandparents fleeing Turkey and then Greece. I thought of my parents fleeing Egypt. Like Lot's wife, they all had to leave everything familiar behind. Julia even had to leave her husband behind. And once our team was at the border, so did Liliia and Yuliia. Every time Julia might have wanted to look back and stop, she had to keep going. For herself, for her children, and for her team. With one phone call, her life changed. With Andreas and Tony guiding her, essentially holding her hand, she and the rest of our team ran for their lives.

Looking at Lot's wife with Julia in mind, I can imagine Lot's wife having deep-seated feelings. It's no wonder she looked back *longingly*. Maybe *how* she looked back has as much to do with it as the mere fact that she looked back at all.

To look back longingly is to look back with a yearning desire.[13] What was it she longed for exactly? What did she so deeply desire? Putting myself in her shoes, I can imagine any number of things. Maybe it was her home. Maybe it was the way her home made her feel safe and secure. Maybe it was the way she'd gotten everything arranged and decorated just so. Maybe it was the way her home welcomed her each time she ran errands and came back to it. Did she long for her belongings? Her friends? Her routine? Her extended family? If you have ever moved from one city to another, then perhaps you know firsthand how easy it is to long for what was, compared to the work involved in adjusting to all that's new.

Maybe she had a position in the community, a place of prominence. After all, Sodom wasn't an impoverished city, and she was married to a wealthy man.[14] Could it be that she looked back longingly at everything she had grown attached to and was being forced to abandon? She appeared to be torn between what she was leaving and where she was going. Have you ever been there? Isn't this our challenge in everything God invites us to do? To move forward or stop and look back? And not just to the tangible things that can slip through our fingers but to places in time, to memories, and to the feelings those memories evoke. It can be any of that or all of that, can't it?

Maybe Lot's wife was trying to preserve the past, something that's all too easy to do. When we work at preserving the past, lingering in nostalgia, we can keep ourselves from the truth of the present and the pain of reality.[15] If we linger in the past, we run the risk of it becoming an idealized version of what really was. Memories can easily be distorted, can't they?[16] Of all the things that could have happened to Lot's wife when she looked back, she turned into a pillar of salt, a substance that has been used as a preservative for centuries and is still used to this day.[17] The irony doesn't escape me. What's more, Lot's wife became the very substance that Jesus said we are. Matthew recorded Jesus saying that we are the salt of the earth.[18] Perhaps we need to ensure that we don't get stuck in a place trying to preserve the past, where we are no longer moving forward, and where we are no longer salting the world around us.

Lot's wife looked back *longingly*. I have found that if we linger too long where we're not supposed to be, we'll start longing for what we are supposed to no longer be lingering in. When we linger, we hesitate. The literal meaning of *linger* is "to be slow in parting. To remain in existence although waning in strength. It's to procrastinate." And it includes one more eerily accurate depiction: "To remain alive although gradually dying."[19] Lot's wife might not have had any idea that looking back would cause her death, but it did, didn't it?

> If we linger in the past, we run the risk of it becoming an idealized version of what really was.

Are you longing for something that once was? That is no more? That can never be again?

Are you lingering there in that place where you should no longer be lingering?

Are you lingering in a place and longing for what was, all

the while tolerating what is, in hopes that if you linger long enough, you might get back what God told you to leave?

When Lot's wife longed and lingered, she stopped and looked back toward Sodom in an act of disobedience. Then she became calcified and stuck, frozen in time, paralyzed for eternity as a pillar of salt. I'm Greek, and because I was raised to salt food generously, I love salt. But I don't want to get stuck and turn into a pillar of salt. I imagine you don't either. But in a sense, I find that getting stuck like she did is so easy to do.

We can get stuck in:

- our emotions
- our thoughts
- our attitudes
- our opinions
- our possessions
- our plans
- our desires
- our habits
- our comfort
- our pain
- our wounds
- our relationships
- our past
- our present
- our future hopes

There are myriad ways and places we can get stuck, and it is my prayer that as we journey together through the pages of this book, we will discover where we may have gotten stuck and uncover ways to get unstuck—so we can move forward into the purpose and promises of God for our future.

It's not always easy to move on when God beckons us forward, especially when things are safe, comfortable, and just the way we like it. Equally, it is often difficult to move on when we have experienced deep trauma, pain, or suffering and we feel utterly hopeless and helpless. Moving on is something we know we should do, what we often want to do, and at times what we refuse to do, but it remains something God eagerly wants for us. Wherever you may be on this continuum, I hope you will be able to identify places where you are prone to be stuck, or maybe are stuck, and that you will be infused with the strength of the Holy Spirit to take the next step to getting unstuck.

Remember Lot's Wife •————————————•

When God called Lot's wife to go, she stopped. Perhaps she found more comfort in the circumstances that she knew than in the change-less character of the God who called her.

1. Identify three times that your circumstances changed suddenly and write them down in a notepad or your journal.

2. Read Hebrews 13:8 and prayerfully reflect. If you were aware of this truth at the time your circumstances changed, how did this truth affect you and your response to your changing circumstances? If not, how do you believe this truth would or could have affected you and changed your response?

TWO

Prepare Your Heart to Go

Sitting on Catherine's bed, running my hand across the covers, I couldn't help but miss her and everything about her. She'd been off to her first year of college for only a month, but it already felt like forever. Every time I walked past her bedroom the emptiness served as a reminder of all that had changed, and sometimes, it beckoned me to come in and sit a while like it did today.

I missed her smile, her laugh, her sense of humor, her quirky taste in music. I missed her hugs and how she towered over me. I missed our late-night talks, especially when they turned into utter nonsense that left us laughing hysterically at nothing we could explain. I missed her having all her friends over and hearing all their latest drama about school, sports, or boys. I missed her picking up a coffee for me or calling me on her way home from volleyball practice to see if I needed anything from the store. I missed finding late-night-snack dishes in the kitchen sink most mornings. I missed the laundry basket in her room overflowing with clothes, surrounded by all the pieces that missed the basket. I have often thought that my biggest parenting fail was not teaching my kids to actually take their laundry basket to the laundry room rather than merely using it to practice hoop shots.

Looking up at all the photos tacked on the wall, knowing how carefully Catherine had selected them and arranged each one, made me feel a little closer to her. She had always been a people person. The mix of snapshots capturing family, friends, school events, volleyball games, and travels was a wall of fun, a collage of her life, a reflection of the people who meant the most to her and the places she didn't want to forget. Seeing so many photos of us as a family, of her and Sophia together, made me grateful that our family was our priority, that we had worked hard to create memories, and that Catherine became the one who loved curating them.

Deep down, I was glad she was at college and loving it, but I was still getting used to the idea that she had moved away for school. As a college student, when I went to the University of Sydney, no one I knew ever moved away from home; we simply caught the train to school and back each day. As much as I wished that Catherine could have done the same, such an option was out of the question. We live near a freeway in Southern California and there are no trains within fifty miles. Besides, I couldn't expect her college experience to be the same as mine. We were in a different country, in a different time, and she needed to live her own journey. Still, I was grateful when she chose a school that was only a ninety-minute drive away.

I was adjusting, but there were times like today when I found myself looking back, longing for what was, and mourning what would never be again. I knew the juncture in life we were facing. I knew it was quite possible she'd never live at home again, at least not full-time. I saw how we were at the end of one era and the beginning of a new one. Even when she came home for a quick visit one weekend, rather than feel like old times, it felt like a new time—because it *was* a new time. She came and went as she pleased. She didn't ask my permission to go places or ask how late she could stay out, though she was considerate to keep Nick and me informed of her plans.

Of course, I didn't want her to remain a child and live at home forever, and I did work on preparing myself her entire senior year of high school. But despite all the preparation, the pain was still real, and the transition was still hard. Catherine is my firstborn, which means she has always been my first everything, including my first child to strike out from the base camp of our home and start trekking after the unique calling God has for her. When you've always hiked hand in hand, so to speak, it's the most unnatural thing on the planet to stand still while your child sets off—but that's where we were.

In the moments when I found myself longing to have things back to the way they were, longing to have her back home, I found praying was most helpful. Praying for her helped me let go and keep giving her to God. It helped me remember that he loved her more than I ever could. It helped me move through my grief and keep moving on to the future God had for her and for me.

WE MOURN TO MOVE

As the days and weeks continued to go by, I grew more accustomed to Catherine living away. We texted and talked on the phone often, but not so often that I didn't give her space. When she would come home for a weekend visit or a weeklong break, I learned to focus more on the fun we could be having rather than dreading her leaving again—and of course I helped her with all the laundry she brought. I began to notice that's when she seemed to schedule a trip home—when she ran out of clean clothes. One day, while folding mounds of her clothes, I recognized that while Catherine was loving her new season, I had to make sure I stopped looking back at what was behind us so I didn't miss what was ahead. I needed to enjoy the adult she was becoming rather than mourning the child she no longer was. I needed to mourn the end of an era but not get stuck there. In the words of King Solomon,

> There is an occasion for everything, and a time for every activity under heaven: a time to give birth and a time to die; a time to plant and a time to uproot; a time to kill and a time to heal; a time to tear down and a time to build; a

time to weep and a time to laugh; *a time to mourn and a time to dance*; a time to throw stones and a time to gather stones; a time to embrace and a time to avoid embracing; a time to search and a time to count as lost; a time to keep and a time to throw away; a time to tear and a time to sew; a time to be silent and a time to speak; a time to love and a time to hate; a time for war and a time for peace.[1]

It's so easy to forget there's a time for everything—that there are seasons to our lives—and to start camping in places where we are supposed to be passing through. From my experience, when this happens, we're likely to find ourselves stuck. Perhaps that's where you find yourself today, living in a state of mind instead of having passed through a season.

I remember when we moved from Sydney to the United States, more than a decade ago. I had traveled extensively outside Australia, but from the time I was born, Sydney had always been home. I grew up in a neighborhood where people lived their entire lives; they never moved. For example, my mum's best friend was her neighbor for forty-five years. My mum's house is where I grew up, and I lived there until I married at almost thirty. When Nick and I set up our first home, it was in Sydney. Why would I want to live anywhere else?

I'll never forget Nick coming home after an out-of-town trip and telling me that he felt the Lord was leading us to move to America. I couldn't believe it. Why America? I loved visiting America, but never had I considered living there. I would have been more open to Santorini or Prague or Budapest or Paris. Those were beautiful cities we had visited that I could envision, but the USA? Where in America would we go? What state? What city? Besides, we'd just finished a major renovation of our home and I was literally living in my dream house. Everything I wanted us to improve, we had managed to achieve. I had determined our home was where we would stay until I was buried. Our girls loved our home, and their best friends were just down the street. Their school was close by; my best friend was close by; everything we needed and wanted was within reach. Why would I want to move, especially to an entirely different country?

But Nick, with the Lord's help, saw a much bigger picture. We had started A21, and he felt the Lord directing us to move to the US where we would be more centrally located and able to manage our global operations more effectively. It was only after much prayer, fasting, and crying that I finally was able to see the logic of a transcontinental move—that I finally felt a peace from the Lord.

To this day, I remember how hard it was to tell my mum and then my brothers and their families. They were as upset as I was at the idea of what our future would look like. It was evident that I would begin to miss life as we all knew it. I would miss weddings and babies being born; I would miss birthdays and sports games, holiday dinners, and family get-togethers. My mum had reached an age where she needed more help, and my brothers and I shared the responsibilities of caring for her.

Never had I considered that I might not live close enough to run errands for her or take her to appointments.

I remember us telling Nick's family, our dearest friends, our pastors, and colleagues. So many of them tried to talk us out of it. "Can't you just keep traveling back and forth?" they asked. They meant well, but trying to explain further, and at times feeling so vulnerable to what felt like disapproval, was painful. It made the grief unbearable, and yet the more we moved through the transition of it all, the more certain I felt that Nick was right, that the move was right.

With the help of a Realtor we befriended, we finally settled on a place in California, though we'd never spent much time there, and made the actual move. But even then, after months of handling so many details related to the move and going through so many emotions on account of the move, I found it easier to keep wishing I were back home in Sydney, to keep thinking about my life there, and staying in touch with friends and family. I was in one place, but my heart was still in another.

You could easily say that I was much like Lot's wife, looking back when I was supposed to be looking ahead and moving forward. Much like the angel who had her hand, God had mine. There was no doubt he was guiding us, leading us, and making a way for us, but it didn't seem to matter any more to me than it did to Lot's wife, because I got stuck just like she did. I had successfully made the move physically, but because I kept looking back, I failed to make it emotionally.

For the first year, because my heart stayed behind,

grieving all I'd lost, I found myself living as though I were still in Australia, and consequently, I wasn't making the effort to build a life in America. I hadn't really prepared my heart to go. I remember spending much of my time on the phone with my friends back home, sometimes crying at how much I missed them. For the most part, I ignored American holidays and celebrated all my Australian ones, because deep down I didn't consider myself an American. When people reached out and invited us to holiday gatherings, I found a reason to politely decline. As you can imagine, living in one place while trying to live in another only led to frustration, and the frustration caused me even more grief.

And with every visit back home, I felt more out of place there too. Because I was not involved in everyone's daily lives, because I was missing all the milestones they were celebrating along the way, I was desperate to fit in. When I tried to feel as though I hadn't left, I'd take our conversations back to where we were when I lived there before. I didn't realize at the time that I was stuck in pre-move season, but they were not. Soon, I felt out of place in the US *and* when I visited Australia. Because neither place felt like home, it grew even more painful.

It was only when a dear friend in the US had what she called a "come-to-Jesus meeting" with me that everything finally began to change for the better. I remember her being ever so sensitive to how fragile I had become and bravely telling me what I desperately needed to hear. "Chris, we don't feel that you are with us here, and every time you come back from a visit to Australia, you talk of how you feel like they have moved on without you. They have moved on because they had to, and until your heart catches up with your physical move, you are going to be stuck between what you left and where you are going. You might need some time and distance to make the transition you need to make, so maybe don't go back as often. Choose to invest your heart, time, and energy into building your life here. God didn't bring you here to leave you in between. He brought you here to take you to the next phase of your purpose."

I came to understand that acknowledging such endings and beginnings is a necessary step in moving on, and sometimes we need someone to help us see it. I liken it to what Joshua experienced after the death of Moses. Though the final chapter of Deuteronomy shows us that when Moses died, God buried him, and then God declared a time of mourning for Joshua and the children of Israel, on the very next page of the Bible, in the first two verses of the book of Joshua, God said to Joshua, "Moses my servant is dead. Now you and all the people prepare to cross over the Jordan to the land I am giving the Israelites."[2] I can't help but ask: Why did God state the obvious to Joshua? Didn't Joshua know Moses was dead? Especially since God declared a season of mourning for Moses. And yet God told Joshua that Moses was dead and to prepare to cross over, signaling that one season had ended and a new season had started.

After a year of living in the US, I had to realize that a season of my life was dead as well, that it was finished. Just like

Joshua had to acknowledge it was a new day, that it was time to prepare to go, so did I, and only then was I finally able to move on.

No doubt all our lives are filled with transitions, some that we anticipate and some that catch us by surprise, but in all of them are opportunities for us to look back and get stuck or to look ahead and keep moving. Not every transition is hard, of course. Many of them are easier to move through than others, perhaps because they are things we've prayed for, dreamed of, or worked hard for that are big wins in our lives:

- When we finish school and start our first career job.
- When we accept a promotion.
- When we start a new marriage.
- When we blend a family.
- When we move into a new home.
- When we start a new business.
- When we launch a new initiative.

But for the transitions we did not pray for, did not hope for, did not desire to ever happen, there needs to be a season of mourning first—mainly because something has died. What's more, it's important to keep in mind that mourning isn't just reserved for when a person dies; it's for when anything dies—a dream, a hope, a plan, a goal, a relationship, an expectation. It's for when anything changes that we weren't ready for:

- When we move away from a home and community we loved.
- When we change schools.
- When we change churches.
- When we leave one job for another.
- When we become empty nesters.
- When we find ourselves single again.
- When we experience financial peril.
- When we receive a difficult diagnosis.
- When a friendship dissolves.
- When a relationship ends.
- When someone we love dies.

In all the transitions I've lived through, I've learned that just because something has died, God's promises, plans, and purposes for my life have not. In fact, they are still very much alive. I know there are times when life upends us and we have to accept what we don't want to accept, but I have found that if we can separate the circumstances we're facing from God's overall purpose for our lives, then we can have the hope we need to keep moving forward. The degree to which we can prepare our hearts to go, move

> Mourning isn't just reserved for when a person dies; it's for when anything dies—a dream, a hope, a plan, a goal, a relationship, an expectation.

on, and keep laying hold of God is the degree to which there is more room for opportunity and resurrection, for renewal and life in the future. If we get stuck there, then perhaps there's less of a chance that something good can come from a bad situation, or that hope can come from a hopeless situation, or resurrection can come from what looks like a dead situation. Perhaps calling something dead that is dead is how we can start to move on.

NOT ALL GRIEVING SEASONS ARE THE SAME

A few years before Catherine moved out, my mum passed away. She left this earth the day of my fiftieth birthday celebration. Although she had been ill for a while, and we knew she had taken a turn for the worse, when I FaceTimed with her before I went to my party, I did not think it would be the last time I would ever speak to her. I felt confident that we would get to share more of our lives together. After the initial shock, I found that mourning her death was completely different from anything else I'd ever experienced. In the days before we left for Sydney for her funeral, I kept thinking how I would never see her again this side of eternity. There was such a finality to it all, such a foreverness. It wasn't like grieving through a minor transition with the hope of finding something different once we were through it. She was gone and I was left. The only transition would be my learning to live without her, and I didn't feel ready.

Mum was the woman who loved me before she ever saw me, who wanted me, who adopted me, who named me. I deeply loved her, and she deeply loved me, even though there were times when we didn't completely understand each other. I was not your conventional Greek daughter, and in many ways, my relationship with Mum was complicated. She had a different vision for my life than the path I chose, and it wasn't until she died that many unresolved things came to the surface of my heart—things I didn't even know were buried down deep in my soul.

What I came to understand after my mum's death is that how we mourn, and perhaps how long we mourn, is affected by what or whom we're mourning—and maybe all the surrounding circumstances. My adjusting to moving to the United States or to having Catherine move out and live a couple of hours away from home was completely different from when I had to say goodbye to my mum. Mourning her was much deeper and lasted longer than any other grief I'd known. It took time, and even when I thought I'd moved on, it would sneak up on me and surprise me when I least expected it. But that's what grief does, doesn't it? I'll never forget hugging someone who was wearing Mum's perfume, Chanel N° 5. I thought I would buckle at the knees.

As more years have passed, I don't get triggered quite so easily. My mourning season is over, but to this day, I miss her. I still have "Mum" and her phone number listed in my favorites on my phone. I can't bear to delete it. I know I can't call her, but I like having her close like that all the same.

When I grieve, most often I cry and feel sad, and yet, coming from an expressive Greek background, I'll admit there have been times when I've been a bit more dramatic. Nick, on the other hand, being from a British background, is consistently stoic. I may be the only person who can detect when he has a change of emotion. No doubt, the way we express our grief is different for us all. I've known people who grew numb or found it hard to function, and others who were more angry or frustrated. The important thing is to be patient with ourselves and give ourselves time to grieve what we need to grieve.

If we look to the Scriptures, there are allowances and periods of time made specifically for this. When Moses died, God initiated thirty days of mourning. When Aaron died, he was mourned for thirty days.[3] Bathsheba mourned the death of Uriah for the duration of her pregnancy, when she carried David's child.[4] When Jacob died, the Egyptians mourned him for seventy days.[5] And Scripture gives many more examples of mourning.[6] Although I'm not sure why they were all for different periods of time, clearly it matters that we take time to grieve.

When I was very young, each time someone in our big Greek family died, the older members of our family would mourn for forty days. As part of this tradition, they signified their grieving period by dressing in black. It was more common in the generation of my grandparents and my great aunts and uncles, but I vaguely remember seeing it. From what my mum explained to me, it was a tradition that helped people recognize the need to grieve and then to move on, and it let others in the community know that they were mourning. In the weeks following the funeral, Mum said the family would gradually transition from wearing black to wearing charcoal or purple, signifying their journey out of deep grief into stages of lesser grief.

Perhaps, when our mourning tries to keep us wearing black, what we need to do is venture out with some purple, figuratively speaking, though I admit, black is my go-to wardrobe essential. I'm not in a state of perpetual grieving, and I'm not on my way to another funeral; I just happen to wear black most all the time because it is easy for me. It requires me to think less about my wardrobe and more about everything else. My girls have tried to help me change, and from time to time, I have given in to them, but somehow, I always revert back to black. In that regard, I suppose I am stuck, but it's not in a way that holds me back from the future God has for me.

What about you? Is there a place where you're stuck? Is your grief holding you back from the future God has for you? Is there some place in your heart where you are still wearing black on the inside, even though you appear to be wearing purple on the outside? It's all too possible for any of us to tell a tale—with our activities, our expressions, and even our clothes—that all is well, when the truth is our hearts remain cloaked and weighed down in the garments of grief. I find it a relief that God promises to help us with all of this if we invite him in. He promises to give us "a crown of beauty instead of ashes, the oil of joy instead of mourning, and a garment of praise instead of a spirit of despair."[7]

HOW LONG WILL YOU MOURN?

I was nineteen when my father died from cancer. One of my brothers, George, was older, and the other, Andrew, was younger. To say we were lost wouldn't begin to describe it. My dad was kind and gentle and funny. We adored him; he was our hero. Where my mother would get worked up about things, Dad was more even-keeled. Though we loved him dearly and never could have forgotten him, as time went on, we did—we had to— but in many ways my mother didn't. It might have looked like she did from a distance because she did go on with her life, but inside our family we all knew she had gotten stuck in a place where none of us could get her out. For years, she would not move any of my dad's things from their bedroom. Because it was like going into a museum, I avoided her room when I could. If I did go in and try to move anything, she would get visibly upset, as if she were keeping him alive by moving nothing—but he wasn't alive. All our family could do was sit back and watch as she got stuck in her clothing, stuck in her thinking, and stuck in her outlook on life. As much as we invited her or promised to go with her, she wouldn't go on and experience new things without Dad. She did show up for most every family party or grandchild's game or school play, but there were times when it felt like she wasn't as present as she could have been. She showed up physically, but mentally and emotionally she still lived in a past that no longer existed. It hurt to know that she was missing elements of a stunning future full of life and hope with us all.

In the Bible, Jacob responded to the reported loss of Joseph the same way my mum responded to the loss of my dad. "Then Jacob tore his clothes, put on sackcloth and mourned for his son many days. All his sons and daughters came to comfort him, but he refused to be comforted. 'No,' he said, 'I will continue to mourn until I join my son in the grave.'"[8]

Jacob was in a state of perpetual mourning. At some point in life, when we lose someone we love deeply or something we've invested in greatly, we can easily be tempted to do the same. We can get stuck in that place, and unless we purpose to do otherwise, there we will remain.

Sometimes, when we find ourselves in such a place, we need help. We know from Scripture that the prophet Samuel loved King Saul deeply; after all, he was the first king Samuel ever anointed. But when Saul disobeyed God's instruction, God set in motion a plan for a new king. Samuel grieved deeply, so much so that God asked him, "How long are you going to mourn for Saul, since I have rejected him as king over Israel? Fill your horn with oil and go. I am sending you to Jesse of Bethlehem because I have selected for myself a king from his sons."[9] God wasn't asking out of callousness but out of kindness. He was helping Samuel move on.

How long are you going to mourn? It's a good question, and one we might need to ask ourselves, lest we get stuck looking back. It's one that I had to eventually ask myself when Catherine left home: *Christine, how long are you going to mourn?*

Yes, I really did that, but I'm not suggesting that we pretend things never happened or that we move on and ignore the pain in our hearts. No, not at all. But I am saying *move*. Move through.

Move through the place of perpetual mourning. Move through the past to the future God has for you. I know there are times in our lives when such a suggestion feels impossible; that we can't possibly accept it's the end of an era; that it doesn't seem we could ever stop looking back and start looking ahead; and yet I believe it is possible, even in the worst of circumstances, because God doesn't expect us to do it alone. He wants us to trust in what we do know and trust him with all that we don't. He wants us to find it possible in him, with him, and through him. In the hope he is.[10] In the hope he gives.[11] With his presence.[12] And through the power he provides.[13]

> Move through the place of perpetual mourning. Move through the past to the future God has for you.

I HAVE MOUNTAINS TO GO

When the pandemic began in 2020, and I could no longer travel the way I had for years, my friend Dawn invited me to go hiking. I had always enjoyed being active and getting outside to run or enjoy nature, but ever since moving to the United States, my schedule hadn't allowed me to experience any of its national parks or see its mountains or rivers up close. For more than a decade, I had spent my time flying to cities, speaking at churches and conferences, and spending time with people. When our family went on vacation, we typically flew to a destination rather than drive. So, while I had crisscrossed the US numerous times, I still hadn't seen what was outside its cities.

Initially, I saw Dawn's invitation as a way to get out of the house in a setting where it was easy to practice social distancing. Little did I know that it would lead to a whole new series of adventures in my life, of seeing God's creation up close, of increasing my mental and physical strength. What's more, during a time in our world when there was so much grief, so many losses, so much pain, it became a way for me to somehow keep all that from becoming bottled up in me. Getting out helped me physically exert myself in a way that helped me spiritually, mentally, and emotionally. There was something therapeutic about being out in God's creation, in nature, seeing the trees, the waterfalls, and the wildlife, experiencing all the different smells and noises. It brought life and hope to me in the midst of a dark, fearful, and contained season. From the start I had no idea all the ways it would keep me moving through the pandemic season we were all moving through, but it did.

And yet, as great as it was and still is, I found that hiking at my age is completely different from what it might have been had I started it earlier in life. As I'm typing this, I feel every ache and pain and each one of my fifty-six years. I've come to understand there's a price to pay far beyond the park entrance fees if you want to see America up close. I just finished hiking the Grand Canyon, rim to river to rim, and although I can't say enough about how extraordinary and beautiful it is, I can barely walk. A group of us, including Dawn and Nick, took the Bright Angel Trail down to the bottom, where we saw the Colorado River, and then we came back up on the South Kaibab Trail, a total of 16.5 miles. We experienced an elevation loss of 4,860 feet going down and a gain of 4,460 feet coming back up, and the views were stunning. As we walked down through the color variations in the layers of rock, we saw mule trains and historic structures. We passed through beautiful grasses and caught glimpses of birds who make the canyon home. I learned so much, and not just about the canyon.

I've had to accept that there are things my body can't do that it once did. Now, it's easier to accept this than many of the other losses I've shared in this chapter, but there's still loss. When I was young, I could play table tennis and soccer. I could run and fall and bounce back quickly. Now when I hike, I have to ice down every ache and pain. There are times when I have to wear a brace on my arm that stabilizes a fracture, or I wear a boot because I've damaged my foot. I never used to care what kinds of shoes I wore, because I didn't have to. Now I look for shoes described with words like *support* and *cushion*. If you're laughing, it's only because you're not there yet.

Despite all the pain and inconveniences, I know I have more mountains and canyons to hike, while I can. And when I can't, I'll walk like the eighty-five-year-old couple who shuffle past my house every day. They are so adorable, holding hands, not thinking about the mountains they can no longer hike, but savoring the afternoon stroll they can still manage.

Watching them, I fully realize I can mourn all that's aging and stay home, I can get stuck like my mum did and not run to new adventures, or I can learn to care for my injuries and move on. If I keep looking back, I'll miss the rest of my life and all the plans and purposes God has for me. If I choose to keep moving forward, with God's help, I won't miss anything.

Remember Lot's Wife

Looking back longingly can cost us the future that God has ahead of us, just as it did for Lot's wife.

1. I shared that in the moments when I found myself longing to have things back to the way they were, longing to have Catherine back at home, I found praying was most helpful. As you reflect on an area where you are stuck, start by praying the following: *God, I recognize that I am stuck, looking back and longing for _____. I want to be free in you and free for you. Please give me the grace, by your Spirit and in your strength, to take steps I need to take to get unstuck and move forward, with bold faith, into the future you have for me.*

2. When we haven't identified what we've lost specifically

through a transition, we can't grieve fully, and we can get stuck on account of it. When I was moving, it was important for me to identify the things I was going to miss so I could grieve them. As you reflect on an area where you have been (or are) stuck, take some time to list what specifically you have missed (or will miss) on account of this transition.

THREE

Go Knowing We Are Who He Says We Are

"Thank you for signing in, Mrs. Caine. If you'll fill out these forms and permission waivers, and give them back to me, we'll get you back to see the doctor as quickly as we can," the receptionist said as she handed me a clipboard thick with papers.

"Yes, of course, thank you."

I had just discovered I was pregnant with our first, and I wasn't quite sure my feet had touched the ground yet. Nick and I had been married for five years and thoroughly enjoyed it being just us, and now we were ready to start a family. But like any first-time parents, I think we were more ready in our hearts than anything. We certainly had no experience for the journey ahead, yet we were eager to move forward with what God had next.

Placing my bag in one chair, I sat in the next and started on page one. There was so much to read, so much to agree to, so much to think about. Filling in the blanks, ticking off the boxes, I did my best to answer what felt like a hundred questions. From my name to date of birth, to any major surgeries, to what ailments I may have suffered, I told as much as I knew, including the date of my last cycle.

Completing my maternal medical history, I started going down the list for any issues from my paternal side of the family that could affect me.

High blood pressure? No.

Heart disease? No.

Diabetes? No.

Cancer? Yes. No sooner had I written the required explanatory words "My dad died of cancer in 1985," than it hit me. All. Over. Again.

Oh my gosh, what am I thinking? I'm adopted. How can it matter to my medical history that my dad died of cancer? All this paperwork, all the forms I've filled out for years, they are no longer relevant. I've been filling out forms all my adult life thinking Mum and Dad were my mum and dad, and they are *my Mum and Dad, but their health doesn't affect mine. How can I possibly know what to write?*

Sitting there, still holding the clipboard, I rested my pen. *Do I write a big* X *on most of the pages? Do I go back up to the window and try and explain the past year? What would I say?*

I couldn't imagine how to rationally explain that for

the first time in my life, the medical history I had always reported wasn't true. And the medical history I should have been reporting, I didn't know. Because months earlier, just before my thirty-third birthday, I had unexpectedly learned that I was adopted. What's more, I hadn't counted on all the ways it would keep affecting my life. Once I worked through the initial shock, I thought I'd be okay, but since then, there had been some real aftershocks, and here I was experiencing another one.

Fighting back the tears, I wrote the word *adopted* everywhere there was a question I simply couldn't answer. It felt so strange, but it would have to do. After numbly handing the clipboard back to the receptionist, I went back to my seat, contemplating how I would navigate this new revelation. I'd spent my entire adult life remembering and reporting medical information that was supposed to be so important, and suddenly I felt like I didn't have any important information to report. *How was I supposed to know what to do?*

That's when another thing dawned on me. I'd spent almost sixteen years with the idea in the back of my mind that my dad died of cancer, so it was possible that I might too, when the reality was, he wasn't my biological dad. If I were going to get cancer, then it wasn't ever going to be because of genetic predisposition, because there was no predisposition possible—at least not that I was aware of. Putting my hand to my forehead, I felt almost foolish thinking that for sixteen years I'd carried this concern. It was hard to believe all the rabbit trails I'd taken on medical websites and how much sleep I'd lost over the years, tossing and turning, wondering whether the same thing that happened to my dad would happen to me. Breathing out a big sigh, as if to clear my mind of the noise, I leaned my head back against the wall and closed my eyes. There was a part of me that still wanted to know what I didn't know—that wanted to know whatever was true—and my thoughts couldn't help but circle back to my birth mother. *Maybe I should consider looking for her. She's the only one who can help me fill in the blanks of all I don't know—about my medical history and so much more. And maybe I could give her something in return. Perhaps she'd like to know she is going to have a grandchild.*

There in the doctor's office, I began to ask God if he wanted me to find her. If he wanted me to reach out to her. If he wanted me to tell her how I'd turned out. Wouldn't she want to know? I remember telling God that I'd love for her to see the fruit of her decision to have me. Maybe I could thank her and tell her how Jesus changed my life. I'd love for her to know that my parents loved me, that I had two brothers, that I married a good man, that I was having a baby. I'd love for her to have peace if she still questioned her decision.

And I'd love to know her story and who my father might be. I didn't want to cause her any problems, of course, or upset her family, but for the first time, I wanted to know more about her than what little I'd gleaned from the documents the Department of Social Services had sent to me—my original birth certificate and the paperwork from her stay in the hospital. That was it. From those documents I learned her name, that she was single, that she had come into the hospital alone, and that she left the hospital without ever giving me a name. Maybe not naming me made it easier to leave me.

For the next six months, all I knew to do was pray. I continued to ask God if I should reach out to her, and at times, I thought of what I might say to her. I had imaginary conversations with her where everything would go really well, with her readily answering all my questions and telling me why she'd felt the need to give me up. But then I'd have another, one where I prepared myself for the worst. I knew that anything was possible, which was why I kept coming back to what I knew to be true, and at that point in my life, the only thing that was true, that I felt I could really trust in, was God and his Word. In time, when the wrestling subsided, I found peace, and I decided that I would look for her.

SHE GAVE ME A FUTURE

Reaching out to my friend Mary, who was a social worker and very familiar with the adoption process in Australia, I asked her to help me understand where to start. Not only was she willing to walk alongside me and coach me, her knowledge and friendship made it easier for me to be honest about my concerns. For months, as she guided the research process, we discussed whether it was the right thing to do or not, if it was healthy for me or for the woman we might find. We debated how to approach contacting her, and after Mary directed me to speak with adoption professionals, I took their advice.

In my particular case, calling is what they recommended. If I sent a letter, it could fall into the wrong hands; it could be read first by someone in her family and cause problems I would never intend. By calling, and having someone assist me with the call, I could hear her voice and have someone to moderate the conversation. They helped me to imagine how all of this could impact her, how it would be such a shock to her. My adoption had been a closed adoption, implying there would never be any contact between my birth mother and my adoptive parents, or with me—but laws had changed, and doors had opened. They explained that in many cases like mine, the mother often tells no one. The father might not either. Someone like me may be the secret they agreed to keep forever.

Mary was kind enough to agree to be the moderator. I'll never forget staring at the phone on her desk, watching as she dialed the number. Listening to the first ring, waiting for someone to answer, it was all I could do to remain calm. My head was pounding, my heart racing, my stomach in knots. I had been curious ever since that day at the doctor's office, and yet, now that it was happening, I couldn't stop myself from questioning everything. *What if I made the wrong decision? What if this is all a huge mistake? What if my birth mother doesn't want to ever hear from me? What if she rejects me all over again? Maybe it isn't the risk I want to take after all.*

The phone rang a second time, jarring my thoughts in a way that I couldn't help but throw a questioning glance at Mary. Was she thinking the same things I was? Did she think we should hang up as much as I did?

Understanding how tightly wound I was, Mary smiled at me, doing her best to reassure me. Diverting my thoughts to all the due diligence I'd put into this moment, I tried to settle myself. Mary and I had sought God and his direction, time and time again. We had prayed together before she even dialed my mother's number. I had to keep putting this in God's hands and trust him. This was not the time to look back.

The phone rang a third time. That was it. I couldn't take it. I wanted Mary to hang up—and yet I didn't want to keep living in this place of never knowing for sure, of never having all my questions answered, of never at least trying to connect with the woman who gave birth to me.

Just then, the phone stopped ringing, and for a split second, I was convinced my heart quit beating.

"Hullo," a man answered. Was it her husband? Her son, who might be a half brother to me?

Mary, ever the professional, leaned in and handled what I would have been helpless to do. Calling my biological mother by her given name, Mary asked to speak with her.

Moments later, I heard what I had been waiting months to hear: "Hullo, how can I help you?"

It was the very first time I'd ever heard my mother's voice, and hearing her speak Greek gave me a measure of comfort.

To establish rapport, Mary chose to speak Greek as well. "My name is Mary, and I'm a social worker," she said. "I would just like a moment of your time. I'm going to give you a date, and if you would like me to continue the conversation after that, I will. If not, I will terminate the call."

Taking her silence as permission to continue, Mary said the date that I was born, a date my mother would surely remember: September 23, 1966.

To this day, I can still hear the audible gasp that followed. The sudden panic. The undeniable fear. "I don't want any trouble; I don't want any trouble," she burst out. "I don't want any trouble; I don't want any trouble," she repeated.

Looking at Mary, with tears starting to well in my eyes, I frantically began shaking my head. I wanted her to end the call right away. All along, I had this feeling that no one in my birth mother's family ever knew she had been pregnant with me; that she most likely had hid it from everyone; and that once I was born, she probably went on with her life, married, and had other children.

I didn't want to cause this woman any pain. I didn't want to ruin her life. She had given me life, and then she'd made a way for me to have a life, most likely the one she never could have given me. When she carried me, it was a different time with different social expectations and standards. I had done enough research to know that, and based on my own experiences growing up in our Greek culture, knowing how unmarried pregnant women were treated, I imagine that a single, pregnant, Greek twenty-three-year-old in Sydney, Australia, in 1966 never would have been able to manage caring for a baby alone—and she would have most definitely been alone. Women in our community were shunned and ostracized for getting pregnant outside of marriage. My mother would have felt terribly frightened, vulnerable, and out of options. Whoever my father was, he wasn't listed on my birth certificate, so it was clear he wasn't going to be around. There wouldn't have been any government or charitable resources to help her live on her own, much less care for me, though there were places where she could have stayed for part of her pregnancy—if they had space or agreed to take her in. Such places were often called mother and baby homes, or infant's homes, but whatever the name, they were places covered in shame where women were forced to do physical work in exchange for a place to live before and after giving birth.[1]

If she did have a place to live, she most likely would have been unable to earn enough wages to care for us both. How could she raise me? She probably felt the best option would be for me to be raised by a married couple, to be in a family that would accept me.

The fact she went through the trouble to actually give birth to me, given all that she was up against, meant that she was an amazing and courageous woman who wanted me to have the best possible future. How could I possibly cause any trouble for her?

Mary nodded at me and proceeded the way we had agreed

if my mother had responded in any way that showed resistance. "There will be no trouble. I will end this call. But before I hang up, your daughter asked me to tell you thank you for having her and that she is married with a baby on the way and has a life that is flourishing. She is grateful to you and for you."

And with that, the woman who gave birth to me, the woman I wanted to connect with, the only woman who could answer all the questions that I would have loved answered, hung up.

To this day, what I heard her say are the only words I have ever heard her articulate, and when I replay them in my mind, all I can remember is her fear. I'll never get to know what her normal, relaxed, everyday voice sounds like. I'll never know the sound of her laughter, the sound of her joy, the sound of her telling a story. I can know only the sound of what I heard that day, and I can't help but wonder if that was what I felt in the womb. She must have been terrified the entire time. Maybe how she felt is part of why I've had to contend with the big three all my life—fear, shame, and guilt.[2] But without her to answer my questions, I will never know for sure.

ILLEGITIMATE: THE LABEL THAT KEEPS US LOOKING BACK

From the day my birth mother hung up the phone, I could have spent the rest of my life looking back and rehearsing her words, "I don't want any trouble," interpreting *any trouble* as a synonym for my name. I literally could have been calcified like Lot's wife in that moment, longing for my mother's approval, affirmation, and love. But if I had given in to that, all my shame triggers would have been activated, and no doubt, I would have gotten stuck in a place hearing what wasn't true: that I was too much trouble to name, that I was unworthy of love and acceptance, that I was being abandoned all over again, that there was something intrinsically wrong with me, that I was illegitimate.

It's hard to believe in this day and age, but in 1966 I was literally considered to be an illegitimate child. It's so hard to comprehend how the world used to look at children whose parents weren't married, but an article I read explains it painfully well.

> In the nineteenth and early twentieth centuries, the belief that children born out of wedlock posed significant social and public health problems was widespread. . . . As a label, illegitimacy described their collective status as outcasts who were legally and socially inferior to members of legitimate families headed by married couples. Unmarried birth parents and children suffered penalties ranging from confinement in isolated maternity homes and dangerous baby farms to parental rejection and community disapproval.[3]

It pains me to even write this. How could anyone label a baby an outcast? Or socially inferior? All because of their parents' marital status? It's unconscionable, and yet it's gone on throughout history all around the world.

I'll never know all the particulars surrounding my birth, though I've uncovered as much as possible from the bits and pieces of information that have come my way. "In 2012, a government inquiry found that doctors, nurses, social workers, and religious figures, had assisted in what was described as institutionalized baby farming. Forced adoptions in Australia were the practice of taking babies from unmarried mothers, against their will, and placing them up for adoption. Some mothers were coerced, drugged, and illegally had their consent taken."[4] For this reason, I was sent an official letter of apology from the Australian government in 2013.

I'd love to think this doesn't still go on today, but I know firsthand, from my work with A21, that it does, though it's illegal in most modern nations. To think my birth mother may have been subjected to this kind of environment or treatment makes me even more determined in the work we do. I have no way of knowing for sure if the medical professionals or spiritual leaders my birth mother might have confided in forced her to give me up, but I was included in a national apology for reasons I can only speculate. Either way, it did feel like one more thing to sort through in my heart.

And yet, in all the sorting I've done, I've learned that the feeling of being illegitimate can happen to any of us. When we feel out of place, as though we don't belong. When we feel unwelcomed, sized up, or less than. When we feel dismissed, marginalized, or insecure. When we're flat-out rejected or canceled. When we feel we have to perform in order to be accepted—but we can never perform enough. If you've ever been labeled illegitimate—and I would guess all of us have, explicitly or implicitly—then you know how painful of a label it is, and you know how powerful it is. You know how it robs you of freedom as it binds you in strongholds of fear, shame, and guilt.

How important it is then that we learn how to hear the voice of our Father above all the other voices—including our own—and rest in his love. Knowing this in the marrow of my bones is what ensured that I did not get stuck in another moment of rejection from my mother when she said, "I don't want any trouble."

When we come to our Father, he will always tell us that we are his children, he loves us, we are enough, we belong to him, and we are his beloved sons and daughters. In multiple translations, God gives us his assurance hundreds of times.[5] When I read how God feels about us in Scripture, I can't help but feel his unending love. I can't help but feel his attitude toward us. "See what great love the Father has given us that we should be called God's children—and we are!"[6]

Knowing we are his sons and daughters, his beloved, is what he wants us to be convinced of, because knowing how very much we are loved and wanted is what helps us keep moving forward when everything and everyone is telling us we don't belong, that we are undeserving of his love, that we are illegitimate.

LOVED CHILD OF GOD: THE TRUTH THAT KEEPS US MOVING FORWARD

Since my girls were small, and to this day, when they go running toward my husband and wrap their arms around him, never once does Nick reject them. Every time, when he sees them coming, he throws open his arms to welcome them. It does my heart so much good to watch him be a father to Catherine and Sophia this way; to see how he looks at them; to see how his whole face lights up. I don't mean to imply that Nick is perfect, because he can't be—but he does his best to model for our girls the way our heavenly Father receives us, the way he sees us, knows us, wants us to feel his love, and to feel like we belong to him.

I know this might be hard to imagine if your relationship with your earthly father wasn't the best, or was undeniably traumatic, but God is a perfect, loving Father. It's impossible for him to be anything but good. He has no dark side; in fact, Scripture tells us, "This is the message we have heard from him and declare to you: God is light, and there is absolutely no darkness in him."[7] And although the Enemy of God and of our souls will try all he can, as long as he can, to get us to doubt and disbelieve God's love for us, God—who can never lie[8]—has gone on record with his love: "For God so loved the world that he gave his one and only Son, that whoever believes in him shall not perish but have eternal life."[9]

You are not a candidate for God's love. You are the object

of God's love. That is who you are. You are loved by God, and you are pursued by God. And when you or I reach out to God, who is reaching out to us, by placing our faith in Christ, what happens? We are adopted into God's family and made his children.

> You are not a candidate for God's love. You are the object of God's love.

> When the time came to completion, God sent his Son, born of a woman, born under the law, to redeem those under the law, so that we might receive adoption as sons. And because you are sons, God sent the Spirit of his Son into our hearts, crying, "*Abba*, Father!" So you are no longer a slave but a son, and if a son, then God has made you an heir.[10]

I love that adoption is the heart of the gospel—and not just because I'm adopted. Well, maybe a little because I'm adopted. But the truth is, God could have used any metaphor to explain how he saved us or how we became a part of his family, but he used this intimate metaphor of adoption to show us that he actually chose us. He does not simply tolerate us because he has to, but he willingly chose us to be his children because he loves us.

I want you to sit with that for a moment. The King of the universe has adopted us into his family, and that is where our identity lies, that is where our legitimacy lies. We are meant to live securely in the love of God, knowing we are neither illegitimate nor orphans, but his beloved children. The reality is we often outsource the source of our security by making others our authority, by placing their opinions of us above God's truth about us. If we do this long enough, it can lead us off the course of God's purposes and onto a personal quest to seek our value, worth, and belonging from those who can't give it to us—be it our boss, our spouse, our friends, our mentors, our followers, or our kids.

In all of life, the most insecure position to be in is the one in which we have something to prove or something to lose; so anytime and every time we seek to find our security in anyone or anything other than God, we will be plagued with insecurity. Can you think of anyone in your history who has this place of power over you? Who are you still looking back at, desperately longing for them to validate you? To give you their approval? To make you feel secure when only God can?

Maybe you're looking back

- at a father who was never satisfied.
- at a mother who you couldn't do enough to please.
- at a teacher who said you'd never amount to anything.
- at an ex-spouse who said no one could ever love you.
- to the middle school or high school mean girls who shamed you for your body.
- to the boss who gave promotions to everyone but you.

Or maybe you're looking back at what you consider to be your worst mistake, the one by which you're still defining yourself.

Instead of glancing back to learn, grow, develop, and repent, we've grown accustomed to constantly looking back, and that looking back has gotten us stuck—fixated even—on the past. We've allowed whatever is back there to define us, limit us, label us, and trap us. But the same Jesus who came to set us free from the past told us to remember Lot's wife, and when we remember her, we remember the importance of moving beyond our past and into our future.

We are captives when we are on a quest for love but free when we are secure in God's love. The race of running for love is not the race that God has called us to run as his daughters and sons.[11] In Christ, we run from the starting line of acceptance, secure in God's love. Knowing we are his sons and daughters, his beloved, is what he wants us to be convinced of, because knowing how very much we are loved and wanted is what helps us keep moving forward when everything and everyone is telling us we don't belong, that we are undeserving of his love, that we are illegitimate.

Knowing that I have been adopted into God's family is the source of my confidence that I am his child. There is nothing more intimate God could have done than to adopt us, and when we are confident that he sees us, knows us, and loves us, we can live our lives unafraid. We can step out in faith and step into the unknown future fully confident that our God is with us, for us, protecting us, and guiding us. We can face the inevitable ups and downs of life with assurance that God is our heavenly Father, and he is willing to help us—even when we experience the fears that we all have:

- What if I lose my job?
- What if someone betrays me?
- What if this relationship doesn't work out?
- What if I outlive my money?
- What if my kid goes off the rails?

To keep moving forward and stop looking back, we must gain our identity, value, significance, and security from God—and not from other people, possessions, or accomplishments. I know firsthand that this is easier said than done, but it is possible through the strength of the Spirit of his Son who lives in us and leads us to cry out again and again, "Abba, Father!"

Let's remember that we are his heirs, and our inheritance as the children of God is not shame, fear, and guilt, but freedom, life, joy, peace, and hope in Christ. If you are a follower of Christ, I assure you that you are not illegitimate, no matter what anyone else has said to you or about you, no matter what anyone has done to you, no matter what mistakes

> **You are his adopted, beloved, chosen child. He's loved you since before the foundation of the world.**

or failures you've experienced. You are his adopted, beloved, chosen child. He's loved you since before the foundation of the world. And he will not stop.

GOD'S LOVE SEES—AND SHOWS UP

I know from experience, and God's Word, that the Enemy will never stop using people, words, circumstances, conditions, failures, or our shortcomings to send his message that we are illegitimate and unloved.[12] He knows if he can get us to believe that label, then he can get us stuck in the past, separated from the future plans and purposes God has for us.

But none of our stories have to end the way the Enemy intends! God is not distant or absent. Not in our own lives or in the lives of others. He is not a neglectful Father. He is a Father who is present and near to the brokenhearted.[13] He sees and hears us, whatever we're going through, today, right where we are. He is sensitive to what matters most to us in any given moment. And he will help us. It's part of who he's always been.

Remember the Bible story of when Potiphar threw Joseph into prison?[14] When I read this story, I can't help but wonder if it triggered Joseph to think of when his brothers threw him into the pit years earlier. I won't get into all the details of the story from Genesis, but when his brothers threw him into the pit, Joseph was stripped of his sonship, his home, his family, and his identity. When he was thrown into prison he was stripped of his freedom. Everything stripped away left him empty-handed. Everything he'd been through shouted, "Illegitimate, unloved, abandoned, alone!" How could it not?

But God never forgot Joseph. Just like God made a way for him to be lifted out of the pit years earlier, he made a way for him to be released from prison. Then, God elevated Joseph to a place of prominence so that through him, the entire nation of Israel could be provided for in a time of great famine. Joseph's testimony was not one of God's absence or abandonment but one of God's presence and redemption. Later, when he was reunited with his brothers, he proclaimed, "You intended to harm me, but God intended it for good to accomplish what is now being done, the saving of many lives."[15]

Four hundred years later, Joseph's descendants, the children of Israel, found themselves living imprisoned in that same land, slaves of the cruelest captor, without help, without hope, seemingly without a future. Everything about their condition boasted a familiar storyline that sought to break them with the same haunting label: "Illegitimate, unloved, abandoned, alone."

But God heard their cries. Speaking to his servant Moses, he said,

> I have observed the misery of my people in Egypt, and have heard them crying out because of their oppressors. I know about their sufferings, and I have come down to rescue

them from the power of the Egyptians and to bring them from that land to a good and spacious land, a land flowing with milk and honey.[16]

What God said about the children of Israel and what they were going through is what he says to you and me:

- **I have observed.** I see you right where you are and all that you're going through.
- **I have heard.** I hear your cry for help. I know you want to move on from where you are.
- **I know.** I'm aware of your suffering, where you're stuck, and what you're feeling.
- **I have come down to rescue.** That's what our heavenly Father does for us.[17]

The next time the Enemy tries to label you illegitimate—unloved and unwanted—don't accept the label. Don't accept the lie. If you or I do—because of where we have been, or because of what we have done, or because of what has happened to us—we will find ourselves looking back and living in the past, stuck like Lot's wife was. But that is not who we are, and that is not what we are made for. God has not called us to a hopeless past but to a hopeful future in him. He has adopted us into his family, made us his daughters and sons, and wants us to live secure in his everlasting, never-ending love for us.

Remember Lot's Wife •────────────────────────•

Lot's wife's response to God's call makes me wonder if she was unconvinced of God's love for her.

1. Why does a lack of confidence in God's love for us lead us to hesitate in response to (or even reject) God's call to do something difficult?
2. Reflect on three difficult changes that God has called you to make over time. Write these down and then capture how you responded. Did you disobey, obey eventually, or obey immediately? What do your responses reveal about your confidence and security in God's love for you?

As you look at your answers above, take time to pray:

God, thank you for loving me and saving me. I want to be rooted in your love. Please help me receive and rest in your love in greater measure.

PART TWO

Strategies for Moving Forward

FOUR

Go to Grow

Standing on the top row of bleachers, waiting my turn to move farther into the aisle and descend the stairs back down onto the stage, I was singularly focused. *Christine, do not fall.* I had made it safely coming up the stairs when I processed in with the rest of my classmates for our graduation, but now I had to make my first descent. Looking down at the steps as opposed to looking up at them felt far more ominous than I had expected. *Oh God, help me.*

They shouldn't be so daunting to me, I reasoned, *especially since I can climb mountains fearlessly—well, almost fearlessly—* but I knew that mastering steps that are completely open underneath, while wearing a pair of pumps, is a balancing technique I've been known to fail—epically. I couldn't wait to walk across the platform to be hooded and receive my diploma for my master's in evangelism and leadership from Wheaton College, but I wasn't sure about getting past the intimidating steps. Along with fifty-six other women from our first three Propel cohorts, I had completed four years of lectures, research, finals, and writing papers to make it to this momentous occasion. I was genuinely thrilled to be here, and I probably looked perfectly fine to everyone watching, but on the inside, I couldn't settle down. All I could think about was not falling. I was besieged with memories of the last time I graduated, some thirty-three years earlier when I received my bachelor's in English from the University of Sydney. I promise you that it was one for the books.

Along with my classmates, I had walked into the Great Hall. Designed to mirror the Tudor Gothic–style seen in England's London Guildhall, the Little Banqueting House in Hampton Court Palace, and Westminster Hall, it was built between 1855 and 1859 as part of the university's quadrangle design. Complete with stained glass windows, gables, and angels sitting on beams high above holding symbols that referenced the arts and sciences, it was a sight to behold.[1] It was there, in a place that almost commands holy reverence, that I unexpectedly found myself splayed on the floor in the most awkward position. How could I not at least consider that it might happen again? I'm not known for trying to be classy. I'm known for tackling what's in front of me and what's next in my life. Ballet was never my thing. I've always preferred to hike and bike and box and run. I did not want to fall like that ever again.

Back then, I proudly walked across the stage to receive

my undergraduate degree, only to shake hands with the president of the university and exit stage left by tumbling down the entire flight of stairs—right in front of thousands of people. And when I say I fell down the entire flight of stairs, I really did. I didn't trip and catch myself. I didn't stumble and experience a great save. No, I took every step with flailing body parts, skipping the use of my feet entirely. When I landed on the floor, splayed at the bottom of the stairs, out of sheer embarrassment, I quickly stood up. I suppose it was a natural reaction, but to my surprise, all the people who might have half-heartedly cheered for me receiving my diploma were suddenly going wild with applause. I remember being completely disoriented and equally terrified but laughing hysterically. Maybe I was in shock. I don't know, but when I realized everyone was for me, and in quite an uproar over it all, I determined to make the most of it and keep moving. So, being my truest self, I hammed it up. What else was I to do? I seriously could have chosen to cry and run out of the building in hysterics, but there are times to just own something and turn it in to a bit of fun. If nothing else, I gave everyone a good laugh and I probably made history. Who else can claim they fell and popped right back up at their graduation in the Great Hall? For all I know, I might have been the most memorable part of the entire ceremony.

But standing in the bleachers behind the faculty members of Wheaton, and facing everyone's friends and family in the audience, was an entirely different matter. I needed to be dignified. I needed to be an example. I was older and more mature, and besides all that, I don't pop back up quite as fast as I once did. More importantly, I was at a historic college, a school founded by evangelical abolitionists, that once was a stop on the Underground Railroad, and I absolutely did not want a repeat performance of what happened at my last graduation. I didn't want to embarrass myself, or my colleagues, or the staff at the college. I was in the first Propel cohort to graduate, and as much as I'm all for making history, that was not the kind of history I wanted to make. Besides, the last thing I wanted was for my lack of gracefulness to be the focus.

Moving out of my row and onto the stairs, following the person in front of me, I began my descent.

If only I'd worn my combat boots or my hiking boots. Maybe they would have helped me have even more sure footing. Maybe I should have worn my sneakers. Jesus, please get me through this.

Making it onto the stage, stealing glances at all the friends and family gathered, I waited my turn, but not for long.

"Christine Caine," a professor's voice boomed for me to begin walking.

Smiling big, staring straight ahead, I moved across the stage with my hood in hand. Reaching Dr. Scott Moreau, academic dean of Wheaton College Graduate School and professor of intercultural studies, in the center of the stage, I handed it to him and turned around for him to place it over my head. When he placed both hands on my shoulders, signaling for me to move on, all I could think was *one down, one to go.*

Walking a few steps more to Dr. Philip Ryken, president of Wheaton College, I extended my right hand to shake his hand while accepting my diploma with my left. Pausing briefly for the flash of a camera, I was relieved that everything had gone just like it was supposed to. Now for my grand finale.

Moving past the seated faculty, still staring straight ahead, concentrating solely on my feet, I started back up the bleachers. Feeling each step intentionally, planting each foot firmly, I processed all the way back to my seat without one misstep. I did it! I graduated *and* I didn't fall! What an accomplishment! I wanted to cry. I wanted to break out in a praise dance. I wanted to leap like a gazelle. Well, maybe not that, but I was so overcome with joy that I had not repeated history and that I had overcome such a nerve-racking moment. Why do such innocent mistakes dog our steps (pun intended) through life? It was a stumble. A tumble. Probably everyone at my first college graduation has long forgotten it, but I was still carrying the memory. Why do we do such things to ourselves?

GROWING, LEARNING, AND CHANGING

Going to grad school was the fulfillment of a long-term desire of mine. I have always been committed to learning and growing, but for many years, obligating myself to a formal academic program was not possible. Like so many women, between getting married, starting a family, and working full-time, my plate was full. I simply did not have the time in my schedule to attend classes, conduct research, complete assignments, or write papers. But when I turned fifty and my girls were practically grown, I knew I could make space in my schedule to go. There's something about hitting midlife that causes you to assess and evaluate everything. I knew that I had less time ahead of me than I did behind me, and I sensed a renewed urgency to ensure I was continuing to grow, learn, and change—all for the sake of continuing to do what God had called me to do in a world that was ever-changing.

I knew that I did not want to get stuck doing what I had always done in the way I had always done it, and I knew that hitting this midpoint in life was crucial, that the decisions I made would largely determine the trajectory of the rest of my life. Over the years, I had spoken with too many women older than me who had expressed regret at not taking more risks as they aged and at not making the second half of their life count in more meaningful ways. They warned me from their own experiences how easily we can get stuck in predictable patterns and routines, familiar habits and relationships and ways of thinking, ultimately seeking our own comfort over fruitfulness in the kingdom. Many had expressed deep regret that they had wasted years that could have been spent pouring out lifelong, hard-earned knowledge, wisdom, and skills into the next generation. They had devalued the wisdom they'd accrued and the contributions they could make, subsequently stopping before they were actually finished.

These stories made me sad and determined to keep moving forward. I did not want to get stuck spending the second half of my life talking about how good the first half was, or constantly reliving my mistakes, regrets, failures, disappointments, or missed opportunities. I did not want to get stuck thinking my best days were behind me and not ahead of me. I wanted to keep moving on with passion into the purposes of God for my life; I wanted to continue to be a faithful disciple of Jesus for as long as I was alive on this earth—and a disciple is always learning and growing, because that's what the word *disciple* means.[2] In one form or another, it's seen in both the Old and New Testament, but in the New Testament, it refers specifically to the people who followed Jesus and learned from him. As far as I am aware, I am still breathing, still following Jesus, still eager to learn from him, and still eager to become more like him. Of all people, disciples of Jesus ought to be lifelong learners. None of us "arrive" this side of eternity. All of us have areas in our lives where we need to keep learning, growing, and being conformed into the image of Jesus.

Before Jesus left this earth, he called us to be a disciple (to be a learner) and then make other disciples (other learners). "Go, therefore, and make disciples of all nations, baptizing them in the name of the Father and of the Son and of the Holy Spirit, teaching them to observe everything I have commanded you."[3]

This is our mission on earth and there's no retirement clause in it. It is not only the job of pastors, preachers, Bible teachers, missionaries, or others in full-time vocational ministry to obey this command from Jesus. Every single one of us who is a follower of Jesus—whether we are a stay-at-home mom, work from home, or go to work as a mechanic, professor, chemist, corporate CEO, doctor, lawyer, teacher, athlete, computer programmer, writer, or nurse's aide—is called to go into the world and make disciples. But in order to make disciples, we must first be a disciple, which means we have an ongoing commitment to learning and growing. There is no expiration date on being a disciple of Jesus—of being a learner—including when we come into the second half of our lives. When I hit fifty, there was still so much I wanted to contribute, but to do that, I had to simultaneously be committed to continuing to learn and grow myself.

> In order to make disciples, we must first be a disciple, which means we have an ongoing commitment to learning and growing.

CULTIVATE A SPIRITUAL-GROWTH MINDSET

I'll never forget the first day I showed up for class; I felt so out of place. Most of my classmates were in their twenties and thirties. It hadn't been that long since they'd been in school, but it had been decades since I'd been in a classroom—since before some of them had even been born. The last time I attended a college lecture, the professor used an overhead projector, and I took notes with a pen and paper. Now the professor had a smart board, and I was taking notes on a laptop. Neither existed when I was last in school.

When they passed out the syllabus and went over all that we needed to know for turning in assignments, I was overwhelmed. I couldn't get over how much there was to learn before I could start learning what I had come to school to learn. In other words, there was software to master, portals with passwords to understand, and virtual libraries to navigate. It was hard to grasp that I couldn't physically go to a library and leave with a stack of books. I can't count the times Catherine or Sophia would see me watching a YouTube video about how to do something online and offer to help. "There's a much easier way to do that," they'd often say. "You know, Mum, you can do that in one step instead of going through all you're doing to get there." They had grown up attending school with the latest technology. They knew all the apps and all the shortcuts. If I wanted to keep growing and moving forward, then I needed to listen to them. I needed to learn from them. So I did. With their help, I built an entirely new set of skills.

It was a humbling experience to realize I might have felt at the top of my A game in all the areas of life where I was proficient, but when it came to grad school assignments, I was most definitely the new kid on the block. I was at square one. I was a novice all over again, and it was so uncomfortable, but I was willing to grow. I was willing to feel awkward. I was willing to look foolish. I was willing to acknowledge what I didn't know and ask for help. I was willing to be challenged. I was willing to look like I was going backward in other people's eyes. I was willing to change. I was willing to be stretched. I was willing to start over in an area of my life. I was willing to potentially fail. I was willing to do all these things because deep down I wanted to continue to bear much fruit for the glory of God more than I wanted to cruise into my golden years, retire, and wait to die and go to heaven. I know from experience, the moment we think we've arrived, we'll get stuck there too.

Psychologists would refer to this as having a growth mindset versus having a fixed mindset.[4] A *mindset* is basically our attitude or way of thinking;[5] it's our mental inclination, tendency, or habit.[6] If our mindset is fixed, then we tend to view change as impossible or think growth is not an option. But if we have a growth mindset, then we're more optimistic.[7] We believe growth is possible, and "through training and development, a person can acquire the skills necessary to achieve the results they are seeking. When there are setbacks, that's okay because a growth mindset understands there will be obstacles along the way. The setbacks offer them an opportunity."[8] With this in mind, a fixed mindset will keep us stuck, whereas a growth mindset will keep us moving forward.[9]

Clearly, we want to have a growth mindset, but as a follower of Christ, I would take this even further. I want to have a spiritual-growth mindset, particularly as I grow older. I want to keep growing in my relationship with Jesus, his Word, and his people. I want to keep growing in wisdom, in understanding, and in discernment. I want to keep growing in love, joy, peace, patience, kindness, goodness, faithfulness, gentleness, and self-control.[10] I want to keep reaching the lost—serving the poor, the marginalized, and those who are oppressed—and fighting for the freedom of those in captivity. I want to keep bearing fruit because Jesus tells us in John 15:8 that "my Father is glorified by this: that you produce much fruit and prove to be my disciples." It is by bearing fruit that we bring God glory.

Ephesians 2:10 says, "For we are his workmanship, created in Christ Jesus for good works, which God prepared ahead of time for us to do." It doesn't say "up until the time you reach retirement age, and then all the good works God prepared for you will be null and void." No, not at all. We are never to stop doing *all* that God has called us to do. I don't want to stop. I don't want to look back. I want to remember Lot's wife and keep moving forward into the promises of God for my life. I want to lay hold of all of that for which Christ Jesus has laid hold of me.[11] I want to run my race and finish my course.[12] I don't want to be finished before I am finished.

BEAR FRUIT AT EVERY AGE

Maybe you're old enough to remember when we used an atlas to plan a trip. Then, in the early 2000s, those GPS navigational gizmos came along that we plugged into the car. Do you remember those? They had names like Navman, Garmin, Magellan, or TomTom. Ours had this buttery female voice that sounded way too flirtatious, which is why to this day I don't understand why it wasn't called a NavWoman. I know I sound old, but that's my point. It's inevitable that we will all grow old, but even when we do, we don't have to stop being fruitful.

Just because we might have to do things differently, just because we might need to adapt to the way our bodies or minds have aged does not mean that our mission, assignment, or purpose is over.

Of course, I am aware that things change as we grow older. I am committed to eating well, exercising regularly, taking supplements, and doing whatever I need to do to look after myself, but there is no getting around the fact that things change as we age. For everyone. Our bodies change, our brains change, our health and fitness changes, and we have to adjust accordingly if we are going to keep moving forward.

Let's face it, if you're anywhere past forty, you probably have an entire list of how you've changed. Like me, you might wear readers and have a pair on every side table in your house. You might even be quite invested in chains that hold them around your neck. You might run to the bathroom far more often and even map out your errands with all the best potty stops in mind—not that I would know this from personal experience. You might require afternoon naps to get through the evening, and my own kids may or may not laugh at the fact that these days, I am often in bed before they are. You might invest in more lotions, potions, serums, and creams than you ever have in your entire lifetime, because things sag, bag, and wrinkle in a way and in places none of us ever expected. I know every time I hike or work out, I feel it from head to toe. My fifty-six-year-old body talks to me. It creaks and pops and aches and doesn't let me do things the way I used to do them. Things definitely change, but that doesn't have to stop us from moving forward. In order to keep going and growing, we make adjustments along the way. If we don't, then we will get stuck being frustrated that we are not who we were and cannot do what we once did. We will get stuck looking back instead of moving forward.

I love the fact that on the pages of Scripture, clearly written in black and white, we see that it is possible to continue to bear fruit in old age. The psalmist wrote,

> The righteous thrive like a palm tree and grow like a cedar tree in Lebanon. Planted in the house of the LORD, they thrive in the courts of our God. They will still *bear fruit in old age*, healthy and green, to declare, "The LORD is just; he is my rock, and there is no unrighteousness in him."[13]

As we age, we do not need to buy into the narrative that our best days are behind us, we are finished, there is nothing left to learn, or that we are done. It is simply not true.

If we are still breathing and have a pulse, then God has a

purpose for us to fulfill. We do not need to get stuck in retirement, stuck in comfort, stuck in predictability, stuck in ease, stuck in leisure, stuck out of sight, or stuck in past memories, past accomplishments, past achievements, and basically stuck waiting to die. In fact, the data shows if we have a mission and purpose, we live longer. One study I read noted that "successful aging is more than longevity or the absence of disease and disability; rather successful aging implies health, physical functionality, and psychological well-being. It's having purpose in life, goals, and a sense of direction."[14]

In one of our A21 offices in the United States, we have a volunteer who has been with us for a little over a year. Her name is Barbara; she's seventy-nine years old and just became a follower of Christ a few years ago. She began faithfully attending church and a Bible study, and as a retiree, she thought it was too late to do anything else. She thought she had missed her opportunity to have any kind of kingdom impact. She has a large family and loads of grandkids that she enjoys taking trips to see, but deep down she wanted to get involved in kingdom work somewhere. After a long conversation over dinner, I suggested she volunteer at A21. She was a little hesitant at first, wondering if she had anything to offer and daunted by the fact that she would be serving alongside people who were the same age as her grandkids. Yet she decided to take a risk, jump in, and continue to learn and grow.

When she first came to volunteer with us, she was a bit intimidated by all the modern technology we use and having to learn about an area she knew little about, but she was willing. Today, she's one of our most beloved volunteers, full of gratitude and enthusiasm, and has discovered that she has a real gift for writing notes of encouragement to our supporters.

All the younger women on our team love being around her. Barbara has such a joyful attitude, is a great listener, and has so much wisdom to offer. She recently told Laura, our global team development manager, that volunteering for A21 was one of the best decisions she ever made. What I love is that Barbara has found joy in contributing and continuing to learn and grow at seventy-nine! Instead of regretting the years she missed, she is making her final years count in a significant way. Having a purpose helped her to get unstuck and keep moving forward. What an epic goal for us all.

EVALUATE WHERE YOU ARE

When I first began sharing publicly that I was going to graduate school, so many well-meaning people said to me, "Christine, why are you going *back* to school? You have a global ministry and have achieved so much in life. You don't need to go *back* to school to do what God has called you to do." But in my mind, I had never been to grad school before, so how could it be going *back*? I was moving on; I was moving forward; I was moving with God. But the whole experience of fielding such questions taught me something: I had to be willing to do what God was calling me to do even if in other people's estimation it looked like I was going back.

Have you ever been in such a place? From my experience, moving forward with Jesus doesn't always look like what we might think of as forward. It doesn't always look bigger, better, larger, or come with more money, more influence, or a prestigious position or title. Moving forward isn't always measured in such ways. In fact, when I'm talking about not getting stuck and moving forward, I am not equating moving forward with our lives constantly moving up and to the right in the way the world often measures progress. I am talking about moving on and into the purposes of God for our lives in a way that causes us to continue to bear much fruit for his glory.

If you were to evaluate all that you're involved in right now, would you assess it as being fruitful? I am not asking whether it is successful, esteemed, coveted, fun, easy, or practical; I'm asking if it's fruitful. What's more, to be clear, I'm not even asking you whether you've been faithful at what you're doing, because faithfulness does not always equal fruitfulness. I can be faithful at something but not be fruitful, but I can't be fruitful at something without having been faithful. In other words, you may be faithfully showing up every day at your work, or every week at a volunteer position, or even every Sunday at church. But have you taken an inventory and asked God if you're being fruitful? Have you asked him what he's calling you to do next that's fruitful?

It might mean leaving a prestigious partnership or your

current position for a less intense one to spend more time with your family. It might mean downsizing your home to have less to manage and to free up some resources for kingdom purposes. It might mean leaving everything behind and moving to a new area where you can pursue other initiatives or opportunities. It might mean giving up what's easy and comfortable for a whole new adventure that you know nothing about. It might mean signing up to serve at a local food pantry, helping kids learn to read in an after-school program, volunteering in the senior-adult ministry in your church, or serving on a mission trip. Whatever it might be, if we're moving forward and being fruitful, then we are bringing glory to God.

> Have you taken an inventory and asked God if you're being fruitful? Have you asked him what he's calling you to do next that's fruitful?

GROWTH CAN BE PAINFUL

With all this talk of my grad school experience, I am not suggesting that the only way to keep growing is to pursue some form of education. No, not at all. What I am saying is that if we don't want to get stuck in any area of life, or if we want to get unstuck from places where we have become stuck, then we must be committed to learning, growing, and changing. We must be committed to leaving our comfort zone and stepping into the faith zone. Within our comfort zones, there isn't much incentive for us to reach new heights, is there?[15] No matter our age or stage of life, we must be committed to letting go of where we are or where we've been, and what did work out and what didn't work out, so we don't get stuck and stay stuck. Instead of focusing on all the things you cannot do anything about, like past successes or past failures, focus your time and energy on the things you can do something about in the present—in order to move forward. Start contributing now and bearing fruit now. It was Jesus who said, "You did not choose me, but I chose you. I appointed you to go and produce fruit and that your fruit should remain, so that whatever you ask the Father in my name, he will give you."[16]

I remember when Sophia went through a growth spurt in her younger years. She would tell me that her legs hurt, especially her shins, but I wasn't overly concerned. I recognized that she was experiencing growing pains. Her body was growing fast enough that she felt it.

I don't know what you need to do to grow, but I won't be surprised if you experience growing pains. The transition from living in our comfort zone, in any area of our lives, to moving into a growth zone will inevitably come with fear, resistance, and obstacles to overcome. It will require renewing our minds so we can be transformed from the inside out.[17] It will require exchanging a fixed mindset for a spiritual-growth mindset. It will require us to overcome whatever it is that we need to overcome. It will require us to keep looking forward and not look back. It will require us to remember Lot's wife.

That same Sophia who was having growing pains was sitting in the driver's seat of the car this week while Nick sat in the passenger's seat and coached her. She just got her driver's permit, and as you most likely know, she has to be accompanied by a licensed adult until she passes her driving test. Right now she's a novice, and after a spin around town, Nick told me how she kept adjusting the rearview mirror and looking back because she was scared that the car following her was going to hit her. We've all been there when we were first learning to drive, haven't we? Nick kept telling her that she has to look ahead at what's coming and not spend her time in the driver's seat fixated on the rearview mirror and what's in its reflection. If she doesn't quit, she will end up running off the road, because just like I learned in my motorcycle safety course, where you look is where you will go.

Sophia will eventually fix her gaze forward. She will get there, in time, just like we all did, but let's not be like Sophia right now when it comes to our spiritual growth and fruitfulness. Let's look straight ahead. Let's determine to keep moving forward and keep bearing fruit. Let's grow to where God wants us to go!

Remember Lot's Wife •————————————•

Lot's wife decided not to go, and as a result, she got stuck. There are few things more dangerous than getting stuck where we should not be, but one of them is being stuck and being unaware that we are.

1. I shared that as we age, we need to keep making adjustments to how we do things, so that we don't get stuck in the frustration that we are not who we once were or cannot do what we once did. Two signs that we are stuck in this way can be passivity—not doing anything because we can't do everything—and complaining.

   Prayerfully survey the different areas of your life—spiritual, relational, physical, professional, educational, and so on. Are there places that you observe either of these signs of being stuck? If so, in what area(s)? What is the next step you can take to keep moving forward in that (or those) area(s)?

2. When it comes to ongoing spiritual growth, there are four primary foes that can tempt us into spiritual stuckness:
   1. complacency that coasts
   2. comfort that recoils because of cost
   3. compromise that carries us off course
   4. a quest for worldly success that leads to us setting our eyes on an empty prize

Take time to pray and ask:

God, would you please bring to mind times of spiritual stagnation in my life and show me which of these foes was at work and what I was hesitant to give up to keep moving forward with you?

FIVE

Take the Risk and Go Again

Watching the video of Nick crossing the finish line of the 2022 Cape Epic race one more time on my phone, I couldn't get over all that he'd accomplished and all that he'd survived. For eight excruciating days, he and his teammate, Martin, had cycled their mountain bikes over brutal terrain in the mountains of South Africa for nine to ten hours a day, all with the intent of raising awareness for our A21 office there. Dubbed "the race that measures all," it's one of the hardest mountain bike races in the world. In my mind, it's the Tour de France of mountain biking.

Together, Nick and Martin had competed alongside professional riders, Olympians, and hobbyists alike to make it day after day, water stop after water stop, medical check after medical check, all the way to the end. Over the course of the race, they traversed dirt paths, rocky roads, water-filled creek beds, and muddy bogs. When they couldn't ride over a path of stones uphill, they did what the pros did. They hopped off and pushed their bikes straight up the mountain. They even carried their bikes when the trail grew too treacherous to push them. On one leg of the trip, when Nick's seat fell off, he stopped, picked it up, and rode standing up all the way to the next water stop.

Though understandably feeling beyond any level of exhaustion I've ever experienced, Nick had made it a point to call me at the end of each day and give me updates. One day it was 117 degrees. One day fellow riders were passed out on the sides of the road and paramedics were running from one to the next. One day Nick stopped to check on a rider sprawled in the grass. The rider had dislocated his hip and was trying to push it back in place so he could keep going. Like Nick, he was determined to finish the race, despite the injuries. More than once Nick had bruised and gashed his leg, arm, or shoulder. Daily, I took comfort in God's protection, Nick's skill and levelheadedness, and the way he's always worn protective gear, including a helmet.

When he'd called earlier to tell me the incredible news of crossing the finish line, all I could do was laugh and cry and shout. Nick, of course, was utterly spent and far more stoic about it, but what he had achieved was nothing short of heroic. It was by far one of the greatest athletic achievements of his life.

When he forwarded me the video our team had captured, I couldn't stop watching it. I wanted to live and relive it as many times as I could. It was truly the next best thing to being there. With my schedule and our daughter Sophia at home, as well as the fact that someone had to be at the helm of our organization while he rode, we decided it was best I stay behind. The more times I watched the video, the more times I saw our A21 South Africa team on the sidelines cheering Nick and Martin, and every single time I couldn't help but cry happy tears. I was so grateful they were all there, particularly since I couldn't be.

Watching him and Martin raise their fists in the air as they crossed the finish line and acknowledge the roaring crowd, I could see the mix of relief and happiness all over his face. I could see the thrill of victory. I could see the reward for all the pain he'd put himself through.

At the same time, I didn't miss the way he dismounted his bike, the way he winced as he hobbled and pushed his bike on down the grassy runway, and I knew it would probably be days before he could walk normally again. Still, I was so proud of the way he'd kept going and going and going through it all no matter how brutal the training, or the injuries, or the relentless setbacks, of which there had been plenty.

SOMEONE WHO DOESN'T QUIT

For the past five years, Nick had spent every available moment on a mountain bike, racing up and down the hills and mountains in Southern California. You could say that while I hiked them, he biked them, though he'd started two years before I did.

His commitment to biking the Cape Epic started one day when I was at the gym, going strong on the elliptical. When a friend of ours named Darren came in to work out, he said hi to me, and then he went on to extend an invitation to Nick that I really had no idea would turn into such a life-changing journey. "I'm doing a bike ride to celebrate my fiftieth birthday," he told me. "Why doesn't Nick do it with me and we'll both get fit together."

That was all it took for me to suggest Nick would do it and for Nick to take the bait. Of course, our friend neglected to give any of the details of what the bike ride might be like, but that didn't stop Nick. Always up for a new challenge, he was all in from the beginning. He did eventually learn all that he'd said yes to, and I'll admit, we were a bit shocked, but for the rest of 2018 and almost the first half of 2019, Nick trained nonstop. What that meant was he began learning how to really ride a mountain bike, not just hop on it and ride down the street. He watched videos to understand technique, stance, and how to handle the bike through the constant jumps. He researched online for tips. He talked with enthusiasts at the local bike shop about their experiences. He worked out to strengthen his legs and arms to master the skill and to avoid as many injuries as possible. He gathered information from every source he could, and he rode his bike hours and hours most every chance he got.

By the time he and Darren arrived in South Africa for the race, Nick had trained for a year, which is nothing compared to most riders in a race so strenuous. To make matters worse, Nick was struck with symptoms of food poisoning a day before the race, just as he walked outside of baggage claim at the Cape Town International Airport.

I'll spare you the horrific details, but he was violently ill for the next twenty-four hours, and it left him dehydrated at the start of the race, no matter how much he tried to replenish his body. For the first two days of the race, his symptoms persisted. Near the end of the third day, he had ridden eight hours in ninety-five-degree heat, burned an average of 700 calories an hour, sweated at a rate of 30 ounces an hour, all while not being able to keep any food or drink down. It was no surprise that the medical doctors checking all the riders at the last water stop decided to take him out of the race. I remember him calling me and telling me that on top of everything else, it was determined that his kidney function was at 37 percent. I could hear the disappointment in his voice, the embarrassment that he couldn't go any farther, the pain that he was letting his teammate down. He had put so much into it all, particularly a year of his life, that he couldn't help but feel devastated.

I said all I could to comfort him, to encourage him, just short of saying, "You can always try next year," because that was the last thing I wanted to suggest. More than anything I desperately wanted him to come home right away where I could tie him to a chair and sell his bike. From my perspective, none of this was worth it, but Nick saw it differently. With IVs and prescribed liquids to get him back on track, he stayed to cheer Darren on. Darren made it three more days before flying over the front of his bike, fracturing a few ribs and bruising his kidneys. But even then, they both stayed two more days to see four other friends from Australia cross the finish line.

By the time he did return home, I wanted to check him into a hospital and quite possibly talk him out of ever riding a bike again, but deep down I knew that would never work. There was something that had been ignited in Nick. On the surface, it was a love for mountain biking, for sure, but deep down, it seemed to tap into who he really is—someone who doesn't pull back from going again and again and again to do what God's called him to do. Someone who likes the challenge of conquering hard things. Someone who doesn't quit, even when the odds are totally not in his favor.

It was no surprise then, that despite all the pain and suffering he and Darren endured in South Africa, they were determined to ride again in 2020. So they trained. And trained. A year later, when they arrived in South Africa, pumped up with adrenaline to have a go at it again, we were all just beginning to hear about this virus called COVID-19. There were maybe twenty cases reported in South Africa. There hadn't been any lockdowns anywhere yet, but all that was about to change. By the time Nick had been there twenty-four hours, the race was canceled, and based on news reports, it was expedient that he travel home as quickly as possible, lest he find himself stuck in some country en route. If you'll remember, borders were being shut down, flights were being canceled, and planes were being grounded. There was a seismic shift happening globally that felt like dominoes falling round the world. Normally, Nick would have flown from Cape Town to London to Los Angeles—a typical international travel route. But because of all the disruptions in service, he was forced to fly from Cape Town to Johannesburg to Singapore to Tokyo to Los Angeles—never knowing if he might get stuck in one of those cities for weeks or months or more.

Meanwhile I was at home praying that he'd make it back to me and our girls, that we wouldn't be separated for the duration of what was to come, that he wouldn't contract COVID-19 anywhere along the way. I was never happier to see him than I was twenty-four hours after he left South Africa. When he walked through our front door, he got a hero's welcome from all three of us.

THE UNREALIZED DREAM

Much of 2020 was spent, well, navigating 2020, and we all know what that was like. With time on my hands, I started hiking. With time on his hands, Nick kept riding. For me, hiking was fun. For Nick, riding had become an obsession. When I looked at him, I could see this unrealized dream growing ever larger, and I knew he probably wasn't going to stop until the day he crossed that finish line.

When the race of 2021 was canceled, like so many events were as the pandemic bled over into the next year, Nick set his sights on 2022. *Maybe that will be the race he will finish and end all this*, I thought. But the more he trained, the more he loved riding. And the more I hiked, the more I understood. We both had a drive to move forward, we were in a new season, and we were learning so much about ourselves, particularly what it meant to push ourselves physically in ways we never had.

For another year, Nick trained. Starting in January 2022, he ramped up all his riding time. He intensified his workouts. He paid more attention to what he ate to fuel his body, as did Darren. But in March, Darren came to Nick and apologetically explained that he had to back out of the race. There were circumstances completely beyond his control with his work that he had to stay and manage.

Where would Nick find someone to replace Darren on such short notice? Someone who was athletic enough to survive such a rigorous course?

It was then that Nick recruited Martin, a friend who had a history of competing in windsurfing, in-line skating, mountain biking, and motorbiking. Martin rode his mountain bike three times a week on average, two or three hours a ride. He was eager to team up with Nick, but three weeks before the race he accidentally broke his nose. It had to be broken again to reset it, and when it didn't continue healing properly, it was broken a third time to be reset a second time—all before they were scheduled to leave.

When Nick politely asked Martin if he wanted to quit, Martin answered just the way Nick would have: "I'll quit in a heartbeat, but it will be ten seconds after you." With that, they headed off to South Africa.

Perhaps you can relate to the challenges that Nick faced during these years. Do you have a dream that you haven't fulfilled, weren't able to complete, or turned your back on?

DON'T STOP

What I find extraordinary about Nick's victory in 2022 is that it was made up of hundreds of small victories he experienced in the previous five years. From the first day he started training, he never stopped, he never quit; he kept moving forward in his pursuit of mastering the skill of long-distance mountain biking. Anywhere along the way, he could have parked his bike and given in to the fear that he would not make it. He could have fallen back on how busy his schedule was. He could have grown complacent and lost the vision for it. He could have gotten distracted; after all, like most people, we have a lot going on in our lives. He could have lost heart, and we all know, when your heart is not in something, you aren't either. He could have felt too old, something that people our age—who are in their fifties or older—often begin to embrace. And when he had to be taken out of the race in 2019, he could have stopped then and never made another attempt. Certainly, no one would have blamed him for quitting. His injuries alone would have justified bowing out graciously. Some might think it would have been wise for him to do so.

But every time he had good reason to quit, he chose to keep going out on the trails again and again—until he mastered the techniques, until he built his muscles to endure, until he increased his stamina to ride nine or ten hours a day, until he learned how to safely make the jumps that rugged terrain demands, until he could persevere all the way across the finish line. Even when he took tumbles over the handlebars or blew a tire or broke a stirrup, he didn't stop. More than once we had to evaluate whether he would need stitches or an X-ray or anything more than an ice pack and bandage.

He once said to me that mountain biking gave him the opportunity to go through new challenges, to increase his capacity, because when you do hard things, you realize that you can do other hard things. I think that we all know what that's like to some degree. We may not be hopping on a mountain bike a few times a week, but we all know what it's like to go through something that feels unbelievably difficult and then to realize that we didn't know we had it in us to get through it:

- When we find ourselves closing a chapter of our lives we thought would never end.
- When we find ourselves as a caregiver for an aging parent.

- When we are raising a forever child.
- When we are pressing on through school, possibly while working and caring for our family.
- When we invite someone to live with us until they get on their feet.
- When we marry again and blend our families.
- When we walk the long road of a health crisis, be it our own or someone we love.
- When we do the hard work that therapy often requires.

All of us have gone and will go through hard things. There is no question about that. The question is, what we will do and who we will become after going through hard things. Will we become someone who shrinks back and plays it safe, or will we become someone who goes again?

I'm convinced there's something about having the determination to press on and move forward that keeps us from constantly looking back. If we don't want to get stuck where we are, then we will have to take a risk to go again to get where God wants us to be. I see it as one more strategy God gives us to keep us moving when all we want to do is stop.

There's a scene in the Bible, at the end of a couple of action-packed chapters, that shows this idea of going

> If we don't want to get stuck where we are, then we will have to take a risk to go again to get where God wants us to be.

again. In 1 Kings 17, the prophet Elijah prayed and told Ahab, the king of Israel, that as judgment, no rain would fall on the land because of all the idolatry the people were practicing. Then, in the next chapter, we learn that the lack of rain effectively caused Samaria to experience a severe famine, and God had mercy on the people.

"After a long time, the word of the LORD came to Elijah in the third year: 'Go and present yourself to Ahab. I will send rain on the surface of the land.' So Elijah went to present himself to Ahab. The famine was severe in Samaria."[1]

Because of the famine, Elijah began to pray for rain. Yes, I know, the same guy who stopped the rain was the one who was now praying for rain, but remember, it was all for good reasons.

"Elijah said to Ahab, 'Go up, eat and drink, for there is the sound of a rainstorm.' So Ahab went to eat and drink, but Elijah went up to the summit of Carmel. He bent down on the ground and put his face between his knees."[2]

Although we are not specifically told here that Elijah was praying, we know from James 5:17–18 that he was because it says, "Elijah was a human being as we are, and he prayed earnestly that it would not rain, and for three years and six months it did not rain on the land. Then he prayed again, and the sky gave rain and the land produced its fruit."

Sorry, I didn't mean to spoil the ending for you, but you probably knew the rain was coming, right? What I want to focus on is what happened between the time Elijah first prayed and the time the rain started to come down.

"And he [Elijah] said to his servant, 'Go up now, look toward the sea.' And he [the servant] went up and looked and said, 'There is nothing.'"[3]

So Elijah lost all hope. He quit. He gave up. He went home. Is that what we read? No.

"And he said, 'Go again,' seven times. And at the seventh time he said, 'Behold, a little cloud like a man's hand is rising from the sea.'"[4]

Did you catch that? Elijah didn't just send his servant one time to look and see if there was a rain cloud in the sky; every time the servant reported in and said there was nothing, Elijah told him to go again.

Elijah: Go up now, look toward the sea. (1)
Servant: There is nothing.
Elijah: Go again. (2)
Servant: There is nothing.
Elijah: Go again. (3)
Servant: There is nothing.
Elijah: Go again. (4)
Servant: There is nothing.
Elijah: Go again. (5)
Servant: There is nothing.
Elijah: Go again. (6)
Servant: There is nothing.
Elijah: Go again. (7)

Servant: Behold, a little cloud like a man's hand is
rising from the sea.

Elijah told the servant to go seven times. When we go again there is risk, but when we go again there is also reward. Like Nick, when we go again with tenacity, resilience, courage, strength, and faith, we may fail along the way—maybe even multiple times—but if we keep going again, keep moving forward, eventually, we get to see the cloud. That's the reward of going again, even when we've already gone again and again and again. I suspect that most of us don't go again, or are reluctant to move forward, because we want to see the cloud before we go, but often that's not how it works, is it? We don't see the cloud before we go again; we see the cloud *when* we go again. Are you willing to go . . . and go again . . . and again?

WHAT'S STOPPING YOU?

God has called us to live a life of faith, and to live a life of faith, we have to find the strength to keep going again. We have to set our hearts and minds to walk by faith and not by sight.[5] But it's never easy, is it? It's so much easier to wait for the cloud first. It's so much easier to let what stops us stop us. Have you ever thought about what's stopping you

- from praying again?
- from smiling again?

- from loving again?
- from hoping again?
- from laughing again?
- from playing again?
- from resting again?
- from surrendering again?
- from starting again?
- from taking care of yourself again?
- from reading the Word again?
- from going to church again?
- from proclaiming God's promises again?
- from finding new friends again?
- from giving again?
- from letting someone in again?

I know the times when I've found myself hesitating, looking back, and then getting stuck, fear typically had something to do with it, even though I know God has not given us a spirit of fear.[6]

To overcome the fear that has attempted to paralyze me, and quite possibly get me to look back and get stuck, I've had to remember Lot's wife and keep fighting the good fight of faith.[7] It's not a physical fight but a spiritual one, and it's a fight we're all called to wage. I've never found it to be easy on my flesh or easy on my heart and mind, but then again, I can't imagine that something called a fight would be. Whether the battle was mental, emotional, or spiritual, I've had to intentionally engage to resist the fear that tries to stop me from being healed in my heart and mind, from doing all that God's called me to do, from fulfilling all his plans and purposes for me. If you know my story, which includes abandonment, adoption, and abuse, then you know much of what I've had to overcome—but we all have a story of some sort, don't we?

In all our lives, there are traumas we don't know how to navigate, moments that stand still in our memories to this day, and those all-too-common reactions to pain that make us recoil and become immobilized. We've all been there, when we've been too terrified to even attempt the idea of moving forward and going again. But at some point, we have to get back up and get in the fight. I've always wanted my girls to get back up, brush the dirt off, so to speak, and go again. Whether they were playing a game, tackling homework, or learning to ride a bike, the only way forward was forward. It was not in stopping, though that's exactly what they wanted to do. Almost every time, their first response was, "Not again, Mummy, not again."

But there's something about *again* that's important for us to grasp. I don't mean to turn this into an English lesson, but even the word *again* is worth examining. The dictionary tells us that it's an adverb; it tells us when to do something. It means "to return; once more; or to return to a previous position or condition."[8] It can be used in multiple contexts:

"It was great to meet old friends again."

"Again, why are you doing this?"

It can even mean "on the other hand": "It might be good to go, but then again, it might not."

When it comes to the hard internal things in our lives, the things we need to risk going again for, I would imagine that we most often use it this way: "I'll never do that again. No, not again."

I'll admit, I've said as much on many occasions—when my heart has had enough and my emotions have run high—only to realize that it wasn't health talking but hurt talking, that it wasn't faith talking but fear talking. And yet I would be remiss if I didn't mention that there have been times when it has been completely justifiable and right to say, "No, not again," and mean it with all my heart. There are some things in all our lives that we absolutely can never do again or will never allow someone else to do to us again.

In my life, because of the sexual abuse that happened to me when I was a child, which my parents had no clue about, I will never, ever allow anyone to abuse me again. I will never allow myself to be put in situations where I could be mistreated or violated. I can't. And neither can you, particularly if you've escaped any kind of trauma. There are times when saying "No, not again" is not a response of weakness but strength, not a response of resignation but resolve, not a response of fear but faith.

Maybe we've had someone betray us, hurt us, wrong us, or slander us. When the Enemy tempts us to rehearse what they did again, to be consumed with what they did again, to meditate on what they did again, to get pulled in the undertow of bitterness and resentment again, rather than walk in the freedom of forgiveness, we need to agree with the Spirit of God: "No, not again."

Or maybe there is an area of life where we struggle with a particular habit or pattern. Maybe it's a way of thinking, a way of speaking, a way of numbing, a way of relating, or a way of escaping. When the Enemy tries to get us to compromise or take small steps to get stuck in that stronghold again, rather than walking in holiness and obedience, we need to flee it, not entertain it. We need to purpose in the power of the Spirit of God: "No, not again. I'm not getting stuck, I'm moving forward."

Maybe God has rekindled our passion to pursue him wholeheartedly, spending increased time in the Word, worship, and prayer. When the Enemy tries to distract us from spending purposed time pursuing God, we need to remain steadfast and unwavering, resolute and resolved: "No, not again."

Maybe God has freed us and healed us of a codependent or harmful relationship. When we see the warning signs of the same patterns in another relationship, rather than excuse or justify or minimize them, we need to find our strength in God to turn from the relationship and say, "No, not again."

The point is, there are times when it is right, good, and God-honoring to say "No, not again." If Christ died to redeem us from it, then he wants us to say "No, not again" to it. If God healed or rescued us from it, then he wants us to say "No, not again" to it. If it takes us further from God instead of closer to

God, he wants us to say "No, not again" to it. We are not called to go again to dead and dry and destructive places, but we are called to go again into God's purposes.

The *go again* I want for you, that God wants for us all, is the practice of getting up again and moving forward from the places of failure, disappointment, pain, heartache, and loss to the future, calling, and work that God has for us.

FAITH IS AN ADVENTURE

I find it inspiring that when Elijah prayed for rain, it was God's promise to send rain that served as the basis for Elijah's persistence. He had one word from God, and he stepped out in bold faith proclaiming that it would rain before there was any natural reason to proclaim rain. The earth was parched, the sky empty. But even before Elijah prayed, he proclaimed what God was doing. He proclaimed what was happening in the spiritual realm where it was already raining. He said there was "the sound of a rainstorm" before anyone felt a drop.[9]

What was the source of Elijah's confidence? It wasn't what Elijah wanted. It wasn't that Elijah said it. It was that God, who keeps his Word, had said it. It's powerful when we start to speak God's Word. It's powerful when we move forward in faith, especially when we can't see anything to confirm our prayers—but that's exactly what faith does. "Now faith is the reality of what is hoped for, the proof of what is not seen."[10]

For Elijah, the length of time it took to feel rain was the length of time it took for his servant to run back and forth seven times. While Elijah's servant was physically going again, Elijah was spiritually going again, going back to what God said.

I don't know what went through the servant's mind that whole time, but I know from experience there's nothing that will challenge your faith more than going again and seeing nothing, especially when it has to do with a promise from God that has gone unfulfilled for weeks or months or years. But even then, in my life and yours, we have to risk going again. We have to risk believing and proclaiming the promises of God before we see the promises of God. We have to know and hope for things on the inside long before we see them on the outside.[11]

> We have to risk believing and proclaiming the promises of God before we see the promises of God.

WE CAN GO AGAIN

Once Nick returned from his victorious finish in South Africa, and after he'd had time to recover physically, we spent time talking about what went on internally in relationship to all he accomplished externally, and I couldn't help but ask him what it was that kept him going on the toughest of days. His answer was a lesson for us all.

He told me that, from all he'd experienced personally and all that he watched others accomplish, people are tougher than they give themselves credit for. He went on to say that if they can push on, they can push through many things. The people who give up prior to having to give up will always feel disappointed, and the ones who keep going will experience the feeling of achievement, something we all want to feel. For Nick, there wasn't a day in the starting grid that he wanted to face another ten hours of cycling, but while he didn't like the process of riding, what he did want was to get to the end of the process. He wanted the reward that comes with finishing the race.

When he said all that, I couldn't help but equate it to our spiritual race and the words of the apostle Paul. "I have fought the good fight, I have finished the race, I have kept the faith."[12]

Isn't that what we all want to say at the end of our race? I know I do. What's more, Nick told me that in some of the hardest moments, he drew courage from the people around him. He saw they were pushing as hard as he was. And when he really did feel he couldn't go any farther, what he really needed was to rest, to stop, and to eat some food. He didn't need anything huge or life-altering. He just needed to eat.

I can't count the times when I've been bone-tired and all I needed to do was rest. I needed to stop and eat. I needed some time with Nick or my girls. And then, I was ready to go again. What I needed was simple, everyday things, and not necessarily a vacation. It's the little things that often give us the most life, isn't it?

Another thing Nick said that has stayed with me is what I learned when I had to recover from a skiing accident years ago. Nick said that on day five, when he rode out of the starting gate and around the first corner, he was facing a three-thousand-foot climb. Knowing there were hours of brutal pain ahead, he said to himself, "I'm going to embrace the pain." It's what Nick has often said when he's faced something hard.

In all our lives, if we don't decide to move on and embrace the pain, then we're more likely to catch ourselves looking back and getting stuck where we really don't want to be. In 2019, when Nick had to drop out of the race, he stayed five more days, long enough to cheer his friends across the finish line. And because he'd seen the finish line, he knew what the end of his race would look like. That is what he kept in mind. That was the vision that kept him going. It gave him the faith and strength he needed to get to the end.

To me, that's what my hope of hearing my heavenly Father say, "Well done, good and faithful servant,"[13] does for me. It keeps me going again and again and again. As many times as it takes.

When I asked Nick how finishing the Cape Epic changed him, I knew by his answer what he had yet to tell me, that he would go again to South Africa and ride once more. Nick said all the years of training, and finally crossing the finish line, gave him a greater passion to continue, a greater tolerance of setbacks, a greater commitment to achieving our family and ministry goals, a greater understanding that if we push on, then we will push through.

So it is with us spiritually. When we are willing to push through the pain of what stops us, we can go again. We can keep running our race and finish our course.

Remember Lot's Wife

Lot's wife was hesitant to go. When we are hesitant to go, especially when we are hesitant to risk again, disappointment with the outcome of past risk is often in play.

1. When we step out and risk, and the results are not what we hoped for or imagined, we can respond a number of ways. Identify a few times you found yourself in that situation and write down how you responded.

2. As you look at these instances, do you see a pattern in the way you tend to respond to risk (or going again), and is there any way that you sense God wants you to respond differently?

SIX

Go With What You Have

Gathering around the tables clustered together, I couldn't stop smiling and saying to everyone how much it meant to see them and for us all to be together in one room. For the first time since the beginning of the pandemic, Nick and I were meeting in person with our global team leaders in Riga, Latvia, for a three-day retreat. In the past, we had always met annually to strengthen the team and forge deeper relationships, especially since we had grown to having nineteen offices in sixteen countries. It had always been a great time of planning and strategizing our future, and with so many of our team having worked with us for years, the love and respect we shared made it that much more meaningful. When COVID-19 disrupted our annual gatherings in 2020 and 2021, it was hard on us all. Since restrictions had lifted and we began planning our 2022 retreat, I couldn't help but expect it to be incredibly special.

Kicking off the first night with a dinner menu of Latvian foods, I took a chair across the table from Szymon and Kinga, our Zoe Church pastors in Warsaw. I couldn't wait to hear all the ways they'd been involved in helping the Ukrainian refugees. Ever since Nick had asked Szymon to travel to the border of Poland and Ukraine to meet Julia, our A21 Ukraine country manager, along with the rest of our team escaping from Kyiv, Zoe Church had not stopped doing all they could to help everyone crossing the border. I had read Szymon and Kinga's emails and reports. I had spoken with them on the phone and met with them on Zoom. I had listened as Nick relayed even more from his conversations with them. And now, for the first time, I had the chance to hear it all from them in person. More than anything, I wanted to fully understand how a church of 120 people had come to do so much with so little to help so many.

Giving them just enough time to enjoy the starters of beetroot soup, rye bread, and herring in a coat, I began asking pertinent questions that led them to tell me one story after another.

For the first two weeks of the war, Szymon, along with everyone from their church who was available, made round trips 24–7 to the border to pick up women and children and drive them to safety in Warsaw. They saw the lines of cars stretching as far as twenty-four miles on the Ukrainian side. They saw the endless seas of women and children walking, dragging suitcases, and saying goodbye to their husbands and sons, fathers and grandfathers, uncles and neighbors, all the men who were not allowed to cross with them. They saw up close the shock, fear, grief, and pain of the women as they stepped foot inside Poland with their children and little else. It was hard to miss how utterly lost the refugees were and unsure of what to do next.

Szymon and his team of volunteers weren't the only ones to help, of course, as there were other churches, NGOs, and international aid communities at work, too, but in those first couple of weeks, it was mostly ordinary people like the members of Zoe Church doing what they could with what they had for their Ukrainian neighbors.

Flashing back to 2016, I was reminded of the time I went to the border in Greece, when refugees were coming ashore from Syria and Turkey by the millions. I found it such a contrast to what Szymon and Kinga were describing. Back then, international aid communities built large-scale, long-term camps to feed and house people, to help them get from where they were coming to where they were going. From all I understood, none of that was the case in Poland in 2022. Instead, there were international aid tents where refugees could find direction, medical attention, food, and water, but it was the people of Poland, including the people of Zoe Church, who were transporting them from the border to safety—to hotels, to apartments, to homes.

Once the women and children began arriving in Warsaw, Szymon and Kinga began looking for ways to help them either stay in the city or secure transportation to family or friends in other parts of Europe. It was somewhere in that span of time that Nick and I started a global relief fund to help raise money for the work on the ground. Szymon collaborated with other NGOs and agencies as he knew it would take everyone pooling their gifts, talents, and resources to provide the kind of help the refugees needed. It was all too big for any one organization to manage, but there was certainly a part each one could play.

With the help of supporters, the church initially rented five apartments. Then, a church member rented more apartments, organizing accommodations for up to one hundred people. At any given time, people could stay in the apartments for a few days before moving on to other parts of Europe, or they could stay indefinitely. More church members stepped up with generous hearts and open hands, collecting or purchasing food, diapers, baby formula, clothing, blankets, anything that could help. One woman used her hair salon as a place for the other businesses on her street to drop off food and supplies. A team of volunteers went to work helping the refugees find housing, secure medical services, acquire jobs, and enroll their children in school. For one family who had a severely disabled daughter who was very sick, Kinga devoted days to finding them an apartment to rent, helping them find a hospital, and organizing therapy for the girl. When the girl needed supplies specific to her rehabilitation sessions, the church bought those for her as well.

Like many Poles, the church members sacrificed even more. They went on to give up their personal comfort and privacy by inviting Ukrainian refugees to live with them. Despite apprehensions they understandably may have had—not only because many of them lived in small homes, were raising their own families, and worked with limited budgets, but also because they didn't always know who these people were or how long they might need to stay—everyone took someone in.

Imagining this happening where I live, I found myself wondering if the people in my city would be just as willing to throw open their doors and share their most sacred spaces. I couldn't help but ask myself if Nick and I would do it as quickly as the people of Zoe Church did. I'd like to think so, especially after hearing more of Szymon and Kinga's stories.

One couple from the church, Kamil and Ania, took in twelve members of her family. Another took in complete strangers, a family of five. Another took in seven, a mix of friends and friends of friends. Every church member offered to share their home with whoever needed a place to stay. Hearing what everyone in the church did, I couldn't help but think of the people mentioned in Acts 2, who sold what they owned and pooled all their resources so each person's need was met.

When I asked Kinga why she thought the Polish people were so open and generous, despite the natural concerns of letting people stay with them that they had never met and had no obligation to help, a glance back at history said it all. Occupied Poland was home to six death camps during World War II. Kinga said everyone grew up hearing about them at home and at school.

"We know the stories," she said. "Everyone hid someone. Everyone helped someone escape. My grandparents had stories. My great aunts and uncles had stories. We read about it in our history lessons in school. When the war came, we knew what to do. It was natural for us."

When I asked specifically about any natural reticence people surely had, she said it would have been easy to give in to such fears, to wait to see what the government or any international communities might do, but in the back of everyone's minds was the thought that they might be next—that Poland might be next.

BY MANY OR BY FEW

The thing I realized after that dinner with Szymon and Kinga was, when they began responding to the humanitarian crisis that the war incited, I don't think they could have imagined the magnitude of impact their small church would have. I'm so glad they never let the idea take hold that because Zoe was not a big church, they should hold back and not do all they could with what they had. Instead, they understood that just like God was waiting for Lot's wife to move forward, so he is often waiting for us to get up, get unstuck, stop procrastinating, stop hesitating, and move forward with him. He's waiting to do something through us. He's waiting for us to put our hands to the plow.[1] This is what Szymon and Kinga understood. We serve a big God who can do unimaginable things through people who are willing and available. Their actions made me think of what King Saul's son, Jonathan, said to his armor bearer when it was just the two of them about to go up against the Philistine army. "Perhaps the LORD will help us. Nothing can keep the LORD from saving, whether by many or by few."[2]

Whether we are working with a little or a lot, it never matters to God. What we think limits us doesn't limit him. In fact, when Nick and I left dinner that night in Riga, we walked away with far more than a report on all that Zoe Church was doing. We walked away with an even greater understanding of what God wants us all doing. If each one of us will do what we can with what we have, even when it's just a little, our little will do a lot, not because of us but because of God. Because of our obedience to God. Because of his faithfulness to us. Because of his willingness to help us with whatever he's put in our hearts to do. Sometimes, when we're stuck in a place, understanding this and then acting on it is what helps us move forward.

I see this pattern all throughout the Bible. God works with our little, whatever our little is, and helps us move forward. Remember when he commanded Moses to go to Pharaoh and Moses asked, "What if they won't believe?" What did God say in response? Did he point to Moses' strengths, skills, and qualifications? No, he asked a question: "What is that

> God works with our little, whatever our little is, and helps us move forward.

in your hand?" And he used Moses' rod.[3] Something that was small. Something that was seemingly insignificant. God used that. And he did the same with Rahab's cord and rope.[4] David's sling and five smooth stones.[5] The widow's jar of oil.[6] A cup of cold water.[7] A meal, a piece of clothing, a visit.[8] Even a little boy's lunch of fish and bread.[9]

In each of these instances, God worked through something small to do something big—and in each of these instances, God gave each person an invitation and a choice. An invitation to participate in the purposes of God where he placed them and a choice to offer what they had for all he had in mind.

God has chosen you and me for this time. He has called and created us to fulfill his purposes in this generation. When we put our little in the hands of a big God, things happen, don't they? Not one of us has the ability or capacity to do all that God's called us to do on our own, but when we give him our little, when we invite him into our lives to do what only he can do, he helps us move forward into all the purpose he has planned for us.

WHEN DEVALUING OUR LITTLE LEADS TO PROCRASTINATION

I find it interesting that despite what we understand about giving our little to God, we often tend to look down on what we might see as little, rather than value it, whatever it might be.

We tend to "despise" it, though the Word cautions us not to: "Do not despise these small beginnings, for the LORD rejoices to see the work begin."[10] What is it that leads us to despise our little?

Sometimes, I think we despise it because of its costs. When something is just starting, be it a project, a business, or our education, for example, everything about it is hard. Everything. And we can be tempted to "despise" it because of what it will require from us—investment, energy, commitment, resources, time, sacrifice, and so much more. If we are not careful, we can come to believe that the cost of our action will be greater than the cost of our inaction and that the cost of our obedience will be greater than the cost of our disobedience—which it never is.

Of course, there are other reasons that we can despise our little. Fear of failure—which is easy to spot because it leads us to be consumed with the what-ifs—can lead us to despise small beginnings.

- What if I fail?
- What if I lose my friends?
- What if I don't get the promotion?
- What if I can't actually do this?

What if? What if? What if? Life can be full of what-ifs, can't it?

Another reason we can despise our little is our feelings

of entitlement: "If God wanted me to do more, he would have given me more."

"God wouldn't want me to be uncomfortable."

"God just wants to bless me. He does not require anything from me. God just wants me to be happy."

It is so easy to allow these thoughts, which can be subconscious, to keep us stuck in a place of inaction. A sense of entitlement can be subtle, tucked away in our hearts, causing us to think we deserve more than we have and that God could not possibly want us to do more if he is not going to give us more to do more with. The fact is that God tends to work the opposite way; he wants us to give him all of whatever it is that we have so that he can do so much more than we could ever ask or hope with our little. If we keep waiting to have more to do more, we will stay stuck.

Likewise, selfish ambition can lead us to despise small beginnings. When we don't want to do what God is calling us to do—because in our eyes it doesn't appear successful, glamourous, significant, influential, appealing, valued, large, or important enough—we can be sure this is at work. We need to repent of our selfish ambition and replace it with godly ambition, which will cause us to see opportunities to have kingdom impact in what can appear to be insignificant opportunities.

There are countless tactics the Enemy deploys in order to get us to despise what's small. But they all have the same intended aim, the same intended outcome, and that is to stop us from moving forward, to keep us stuck, to render us unfruitful. Let's be those who understand what that is so that we aren't outwitted by the Enemy's devices.[11]

When Elijah asked the widow of Zarephath for a piece of bread, she said, "As the LORD your God lives, I don't have anything baked—only a handful of flour in the jar and a bit of oil in the jug. Just now, I am gathering a couple of sticks in order to go prepare it for myself and my son so we can eat it and die."[12]

The widow's focus was on what she lacked. She was consumed by the little she had. Look at the words she used: *only, a handful,* and *a bit.* By the way, did you notice what she said right after she focused on the little she had? She said, "I am gathering a couple of [literally two!] sticks." Why mention two sticks? Was there a stick shortage in the land? Were there only two she could use? Of course not. She was spiraling in negativity. By fixating on her lack, she saw limitation everywhere she looked. We need to learn from this. When we narrow our focus to what we lack, we end up seeing through a lens of limitation—and that lens of limitation leads to procrastination. What do your words sound like? Do they sound like the widow's words? Are you focusing on what you lack?

To explain this a bit more, if we're not careful in how we perceive something's value—particularly when it appears little—then we can find ourselves in a place of devaluing it. We can find ourselves thinking, evaluating, assessing, and pondering what we don't have instead of working with what we do have. Remember the story of the widow who placed two coins in the temple treasury? Jesus saw her and he said, "Truly I tell you, this poor widow has put more into the treasury than all the others. For they all gave out of their surplus, but she out of her poverty has put in everything she had—all she had to live on."[13]

It's so easy to find ourselves hesitating to act and procrastinating to the point where we become stuck, but God never wants that for us. The word *procrastinating* means "to put off intentionally the doing of something that should be done." Another definition says, "to put off *habitually*."[14] I don't want to get stuck ever, and I feel sure you don't either, but I suspect we all naturally procrastinate to some extent when we put off doing what we don't want to do—chores, homework, business meetings, phone calls, confrontations, working out, projects, and the like. But when our procrastinating starts to delay the purpose of God from being realized in our lives, we might need to take a closer look at how to stop it from stopping us.

When I asked our A21 clinical psychologist, Dr. Rhiannon Bell, who works with our aftercare programs and survivors, what she considered to be the top reasons we all get stuck, she described procrastination as one of the biggest. She went on to say that oftentimes, procrastinators are perfectionists, and if someone has perfectionistic standards, then there can be a fear of not reaching expectations, and when that happens, they can begin to procrastinate, because they don't want to fail.

I would imagine that perfectionism and procrastination working together in our lives would create a vicious cycle where we couldn't help but find ourselves stuck and not moving forward. Maybe not in every area of our lives but quite possibly in several. In my own life, I have hesitated at times. I've procrastinated at times. I've even told myself that I worked better under pressure to ease my conscience—sometimes I actually did work better under pressure—but deep down I knew that wasn't true; especially when I put others around me under the same pressure. Still, I've done my best not to let perfectionism—which I can be guilty of—lead me to procrastination, which is so easy to do. I understand that none of us want to fail, but anytime we take a step forward, we can't help but risk failure. From my experience, it's better to move forward and fail than to stay stuck and miss out on all that God wants to do in us, through us, and with us. Each time I've stepped out in faith,

> From my experience, it's better to move forward and fail than to stay stuck and miss out on all that God wants to do in us, through us, and with us.

started a new initiative, or even stepped out on a stage to speak, I've felt the fear of failure. I've felt the possibilities of the risk I was taking. But I refused to let that stop me.

At this stage of my life, I've risked moving forward so many times that I just make myself do whatever it is that I need to do whenever I need to do it. I learned years ago to never get up and ask myself how I feel about doing anything I need to do, whether it's writing a message, completing a project, or working out. If I go down such roads mentally, more than likely, I'll never complete anything again. I'll find a million reasons to procrastinate on a daily basis. I'll get stuck thinking of the next email I need to send, the next phone call I need to make, the next meeting I need to schedule, the next message I need to research, the next paper I need to write, the next plane I need to catch—anything besides taking the next step to move forward with what needs to be done.

I'm not suggesting it was easy getting to this place—not at all. I know my own weakness. I know how much I love fries and baklava and baked feta. I know how much I love to lay in the hammock. I know the power of perfectionism and procrastination to stop me, but I also know God's power, a power that is so much greater.

When the widow of Zarephath did what Elijah asked her to do with what little she had, God made sure it was more than enough. "Then the woman, Elijah, and her household ate for many days. The flour jar did not become empty, and the oil jug did not run dry, according to the word of the Lord he had spoken through Elijah."[15]

I'm so glad Szymon and Kinga did not hesitate like Lot's wife did, because hesitation is procrastination, isn't it? Szymon and Kinga did not procrastinate when they learned what was happening at the border of Poland and Ukraine. They didn't stop and question if they had enough resources or time or space. They didn't require a solution for all the millions of refugees to start helping some of the refugees. They just went. And they went in faith, with all the faith they had, trusting

God that the mustard-seed-size faith they started with was more than enough. Isn't that the same faith he's given to each of us? "'If you have faith the size of a mustard seed,' the Lord said, 'you can say to this mulberry tree, "Be uprooted and planted in the sea," and it will obey you.'"[16]

Szymon and Kinga did what they could with what God put in their hands, and he used it. What's more, because they were faithful with what God gave them, he put more in their hands to do more through their hands. They understood the principle Jesus taught us all: "Whoever is faithful in very little is also faithful in much, and whoever is unrighteous in very little is also unrighteous in much."[17]

WHAT DO YOU SEE? THE ROLE OF PERCEPTION

When God calls us to do something new, to start with what we have, the truth is that we can perceive that call in two ways: either as an interruption or as an invitation.

When the angels came to Sodom on a rescue mission, Lot and his family were accustomed to life as they knew it. There is no doubt they had plans for their day, for their week, maybe even for the year, and we can tell from their delayed response to the angels and Lot's wife's looking back that those plans didn't include relocation. For them the call to set out and step out, starting with what they had, was an interruption.

Contrast that to the widow. When Elijah came, she had definite plans. She was in the process of gathering sticks to prepare the final meal for her family, and Elijah redirected her: "But first make a small loaf of bread for me from what you have and bring it to me, and then make something for yourself and your son."[18] She did as directed, not perceiving the call to take these steps as an interruption but as an invitation.

Szymon and Kinga did the same. Before the war, Szymon and Kinga had mapped out the entire year for Zoe Church. They had plans for expanding their outreach, growth, and discipleship. They had scheduled a church move to a larger facility. But when the war started, they completely scrapped all those plans, because an entirely different set of priorities took precedence. When they made that first run to meet Julia and the team at the border, they didn't know how many women and children they would eventually help. They didn't know the end from the beginning, and to be honest, they still don't. They don't know when or how the war will end. They don't know how many more women and children will need their help. They don't have any idea what the future may hold, but they do know to keep taking the next incremental step into all that God has for the people of Zoe Church—and the people of Ukraine.

When Nick and I said goodbye to everyone at our global retreat, Szymon said to us, "Even if the war were to end tomorrow, even if there was to be a peace treaty negotiated and signed, Zoe Church is in this for the long haul. We understand long-term obedience. We know, even if nothing else were to be bombed, it will still take ten to fifteen years to rebuild what has been destroyed, and we will be here doing what we can with what we have to keep helping the people of Ukraine."

If we are going to start with what we have—even if it is just a little—we have to learn to accept the call to get started as an invitation into God's purposes instead of rejecting it as an interruption to our plans.

GETTING STARTED

Everything in my life started with doing what I could with what I had right where I was. I didn't start with a global ministry. I didn't start with leading a global anti–human trafficking organization or a global women's movement. I didn't start with speaking and encouraging people on television, in churches, at conferences, through books or podcasts. I started with giving my life fully to Jesus, attending church, and then volunteering with our youth ministry. From there, I just kept doing the next incremental step God gave me to do. I kept showing up, serving, doing whatever was placed in my hand to do, with great passion, commitment, faithfulness, joy, and sometimes reluctance and tears. Over the decades, God kept opening doors of opportunity that I could never have planned for, or even dreamed of. There were times when I thought I was moving backward, but God was moving me forward. There have been numerous wilderness seasons, pruning seasons, lamenting seasons, and countless trials, storms, disappointments, and mistakes I've made along the way. But somehow, by the grace of God, and the commitment I've had to keep pressing on, I kept taking the next step that was before me. God is the one who does the building; we are the ones who keep obeying, keep believing, keep following, and keep moving.[19]

Is God calling you to step out and start with what you have, even if you think it is a little? I understand that it's not always easy to take that next step, but in order to keep moving forward, we have to. We have to let go of the old, the familiar, the safe, the comfortable, the known—which is exactly what God wanted for Lot's wife. We have to quit second-guessing ourselves. We have to be flexible, pliable, willing to change and grow. All you need to take the next step is faith that is as small as a mustard seed. What step is God calling you to take to get started? My prayer is that you will take that step of faith today, because a little in the hands of God can do a lot!

Remember Lot's Wife ●────────────────●

Lot's wife may have feared or despised small beginnings.

1. Read Luke 10:3–17. What did Jesus send the disciples out with? Why do you think Jesus sent the disciples out with so few provisions?

2. Reflect on Scripture (including, but not limited to, 1

Thessalonians 5:24; Psalm 50:10–12; Philippians 4:19; 1 Thessalonians 5:16–18; Hebrews 11:6; James 4:3). What beliefs about God and his character, and what practices in prayer, can help safeguard us against despising small beginnings?

SEVEN

Don't Go It Alone

Knowing how anxious I get at even the thought of encountering a snake on a trail, my friend and hiking buddy Dawn walked ahead of me, prodding the brush on either side of the path with her trekking poles. The idea was that if there were a snake lurking in one bush or another, then the disturbance would send the snake slithering in the opposite direction and far away from where we had to step next. Having hiked together consistently for a couple of years, Dawn had been more than gracious to take on this role of scaring away the snakes. While I loved hiking and appreciated the wonders of nature, I did not like snake encounters. Dawn didn't either, of course, but having hiked decades longer than me, she took it all in stride; after all, we both knew that it was their habitat, not ours—something that was made perfectly clear on the sign posted at the trailhead. In big bold letters it warned, Beware of Rattlesnakes. In fact, such signs were posted at the beginning of most trails in Southern California. On every hike we'd trekked, it was all I could do to walk past those signs and not start obsessing about the possibility of seeing a snake. Dawn was great to start conversations that distracted me, and they always helped to keep me at ease.

Today's hike was up Mount Baden-Powell, one of California's tallest peaks in the San Gabriel Mountains, reaching a summit of 9,356 feet and named after Robert Baden-Powell, founder of the World Organization of the Scout movement. From the trailhead, it's an elevation gain of about 2,800 feet, five hours of hiking, and eight miles round trip. It wasn't my first time up the mountain, but with that kind of gain, there are altitude changes that even the most seasoned hiker has to manage. Noticing my stamina starting to wane a bit, Dawn offered a promise of respite, "Not too much farther, Chris, and we'll stop to rest. You got this! Remember?"

I was doing my best to take her encouragement to heart and couldn't help but appreciate the words she chose to move me forward. "You got this!" was the universal way of telling a fellow hiker that they were going to be okay, they could do it, and despite all the pain and suffering they might be feeling, making it to the top was going to be worth it.

Having made it to the top of so many other mountains, I totally believed it, but today, at that particular point on the trail, I was starting to have my doubts. I couldn't help being more focused on not dying than reaching the summit. Between enduring the excessive heat, my legs cramping, adjusting to the altitude, and managing my anxiety about possibly seeing a snake, I just wanted to stop and call Nick to send the rescue team to airlift me to safety.

To this day, I'm not sure what happened next exactly, but I almost did need the rescue team. In a matter of minutes, someone walking down the trail alerted us that she'd seen a rattlesnake crossing the path at the next bend. Most likely, the snake would have been long gone by the time we got to the bend, but my imagination got the best of me. I became so terrified at the thought of meeting up with it, I began to pray aloud, and then I started running through that section of the path. Before I knew it, I hit myself with my own trekking poles, bruised my leg, hurt my arm, pulled a calf muscle, and fell to the ground. Who needs the threat of a snake when you have skills like I do? By the time I landed, I was covered in scratches and utterly shaken inside and out. I remember grabbing my arm first, but because of the gripping pain in my calf, I quickly moved to nurse my leg, doing all I knew to make the muscle relax and let me continue hiking. When the muscle wouldn't relax, I grew genuinely concerned that I wasn't going to make it off the mountain. Embarrassed, exhausted, and angry at myself—and the snake—I tried to calm down. I had done all this to myself because of the *perceived* threat of a snake—not the reality of a snake—and my ego hurt as much as the rest of me.

Dawn was quick to get to me and begin assessing my injuries. Seeing my struggle, a few more hikers who had been following us stopped to render aid. Along with Dawn, they began pulling supplies out of their packs—supplements, energy bars, a compression wrap, and more hydration. They knew exactly what my calf muscle was doing, and they knew how to help. I love this about the hiking community. Everyone is so kind, generous, and has each other's back because we all know we could be the next one to run out of water, get injured, or take a tumble. I gratefully took all their advice, and gradually, I began to feel my muscle calming down. When we all felt reassured that I'd be okay and get off the mountain alive—and by my own volition—they began gathering up their packs to head on up the trail. I couldn't help but smile when one by one they offered me a fist bump and said, "You got this!"

Ever since Dawn had invited me to start hiking in early 2020, she'd been diligent to teach me everything she knew about it. She had taught me critical information like when you're hiking back down a narrow trail, always yield to hikers coming up the trail, because they have the right of way. She taught me the names of different kinds of trails; for instance, when a trail zigzags back and forth on a mountainside, it's called a switchback. Even in the days leading up to a hike, she was invaluable in teaching me how to prepare. She would often text me reminders of when to exercise and when to rest, what to eat and when to eat it, what supplements to take to ease any altitude sickness, and go the distance. Of all she taught me, the greatest advice was when going on a long hike, never go it alone; always have a hiking buddy. "You never know what may happen on a trail," she said, "and having someone with you can make all the difference in making it to the top and getting back down safely."

That advice proved true countless times, including that day as I stressed about encountering the rattlesnake.

"Think you're ready to keep going?" Dawn asked.

"Yes, let's do this!" I said with far more enthusiasm than I felt.

Helping me to my feet, Dawn took the lead once more. Though I kept up the pace, I found myself limping much of the day to manage the pain. There's no way I could have made it without Dawn. Watching her prodding the bushes like always, I couldn't help but think that we shouldn't go it alone, not only when we hike but also as we trek through life. "Two are better than one," Scripture says, "because they have a good reward for their efforts. For if either falls, his companion can lift him up; but pity the one who falls without another to lift him up."[1]

If we are to keep moving forward into all the plans and purposes God has for us, then we can't go it alone. We can't do what God has called us to do by ourselves. And yet, for one reason or another, we often try to do it alone, don't we? I know I do at times. It seems ingrained in us to be independent, to prove we can make it on our own in this life, but God didn't design us to operate that way. He placed us in a body and exhorted us to carry one another's burdens,[2] to care for each other's practical needs,[3] to warn each other of sin,[4] and to rejoice and mourn with one another.[5] We can't do any of these things if we're not involved in each other's lives and supporting one another. Good friendships and strong relationships are a crucial component in helping us to keep moving forward in life.

FRIENDS ARE GOD'S PLAN

Dawn and I have been hiking buddies for only the past few years, but we have been good friends for almost twenty-five years, ever since I made one of my first ministry trips to the United States, back when I lived in Australia. We met after the church where she served as a youth pastor invited me to speak. Only a few months apart in age, and both with a passion for the next generation, we hit it off right away. Through the years, as I was invited to speak at her church again and again, we'd grab a coffee and catch up on our lives, often sharing what God was doing and how we were moving through everything life was throwing our way. We were women in frontline ministry, something that wasn't as common twenty-five years ago as it is today. I'm so grateful things have changed since then, but early in our

> Good friendships and strong relationships are a crucial component in helping us to keep moving forward in life.

ministry lives we didn't have many role models to look to, talk to, and learn from, so we learned from each other. When we got together, we talked about what it was like to be single and in ministry, as Dawn was single and I had spent much of my twenties being single, traveling and speaking to youth. We talked about navigating our leadership roles in rooms where most leaders were men, and how to fulfill all that God had put in us to do. Of course, we talked about everything else under the sun, too, but having someone to talk to about our callings meant so much.

Though I was married and later had two children, Dawn remained single and got two dogs. I knew she wanted to be married—and she still does—but she was not going to put her life and calling on hold waiting for that day. Instead she chose to be obedient to God and trust him with her relational future, while still moving forward. Rather than get stuck in disappointment or keep looking back at how many weddings she had attended, she kept showing up in her own life and filling it with purpose. She built great friendships, took up running and hiking, bought a house, went to grad school, and kept stepping into new positions in her calling. She kept pressing on, knowing that her completion was in Christ and that he had a plan and purpose for her that was good.

Today, Dawn and I not only hike together but she is now the executive director of our ministry, Equip & Empower. So we are not only friends but also work colleagues and ministry compadres who are moving forward into more of what

God wants to do in us and through us. Even at my age, and especially at my age, I do not want to do this life alone. I'm in the second half of life and ministry and I want to run hard alongside people who are running hard toward Jesus. I need encouragement. I need inspiration. I need accountability. I need people who get it, and Dawn is definitely one of those friends.

GOD PUTS PEOPLE TOGETHER

I'm so glad God has a way of putting people together for his glory and for their mutual benefit. In fact, it's something we see throughout the Bible. In story after story, we see people who are relatives, who are acquaintances, who are from different generations, who are thrown together because of mission, and what we observe is that because they come into alliance with one another, because they become friends, they are cared for, rescued, delivered, and fulfill what it is they were put on this earth to do. Because they stick together, they continue to move forward in instances where it would have been impossible for them to do so on their own.

Do you remember the Bible story where Aaron and Hur held up Moses' arms when he no longer had the strength to do it himself? The Amalekites had attacked Israel, and while Joshua fought the battle on the ground, Moses fought the battle from high on a hilltop.

DON'T GO IT ALONE

While Moses held up his hand, Israel prevailed, but whenever he put his hand down, Amalek prevailed. When Moses's hands grew heavy, they took a stone and put it under him, and he sat down on it. Then Aaron and Hur supported his hands, one on one side and one on the other so that his hands remained steady until the sun went down. So Joshua defeated Amalek and his army with the sword.[6]

What any of them never could have accomplished separately, they did by coming together. They won the battle by being better together.

Consider the relationship between Joshua and Caleb. When Moses picked a leader from each tribe to go and spy out the promised land, Joshua and Caleb were the only ones to come back with a positive report. When the people chose to believe the other ten spies and turn against Joshua and Caleb, Moses intervened, and years later they became the only two of their generation to enter the promised land. Through circumstances that God orchestrated, they went from slaves to spies to co-laborers who took a nation into Canaan.

Naomi and Ruth are another pair that God brought together. Though they began as a mother-in-law and a daughter-in-law who then became widows, they grew into lifelong companions. When Naomi told Ruth and her other daughter-in-law to stay in their homeland and find new husbands, it was Ruth who said, "Don't plead with me to abandon you or to return and not follow you. For wherever you go, I will go, and wherever you live, I will live; your people will be my people, and your God will be my God."[7] Because of Ruth's loyalty, Naomi and Ruth's journey of sticking together took them to a place that secured both their futures. If you're familiar with their friendship, then you know that Ruth eventually married Boaz, but she never left Naomi behind. And when she and Boaz had a son, it was Naomi who cared for their child.[8]

Perhaps one of the most famous duos in the Bible is David and Jonathan. From the first time they met, after David had killed the giant Goliath and was brought before Jonathan's father, King Saul, David and Jonathan bonded as friends and as brothers. "When David had finished speaking with Saul, Jonathan was bound to David in close friendship, and loved him as much as he loved himself."[9] In the years to come Jonathan saved David's life, not once, but twice. When they devised a plan to spare David's life a second time, it involved David going away and Jonathan remaining with King Saul. Scripture tells us they wept with each other, though David wept more.[10] Although Jonathan was heir to the throne, Jonathan did not cling to his position but sacrificed his rights and his claim to support the calling and anointing of God on David. Because of their loyal friendship, David went on to become the king he'd been anointed to be, something that secured the lineage of Jesus.

Clearly, God puts people together on purpose for a purpose. After Paul was transformed and began ministering the gospel throughout the known world, Scripture lists as many as forty men and women who traveled with him, preached with him, fellowshipped with him, ate with him, and supported him financially.[11] Paul mentioned many of them by name in his writings.[12] He didn't go it alone. There was Phoebe, Barnabas, John Mark, Mary, Onesimus, Silas, Lydia, Urbanus, Priscilla, Aquila, and Philemon, to name a few.[13] It was Timothy who became his protégé and then his colleague. When Paul wrote to the Philippians, he said,

> Now I hope in the Lord Jesus to send Timothy to you soon so that I too may be encouraged by news about you. For I have no one else like-minded who will genuinely care about your interests; all seek their own interests, not those of Jesus Christ. But you know his proven character, because he has served with me in the gospel ministry like a son with a father.[14]

JESUS CALLS US FRIEND

Even when Jesus walked this earth, he didn't go it alone. God put him together with the apostles, and then with the rest of his disciples—and when Jesus sent the disciples out, he sent them two by two.[15] Within the group of apostles, an inner circle formed—Peter, James, and John.[16] And in that circle, it was John who described himself as "the one Jesus loved."[17] It was John whom Jesus entrusted his mother to before he took his last breath.[18]

Outside that inner circle, there were men and women who supported Jesus' ministry with their own means and traveled with him.[19] There were apostles and friends like Matthew, Judas, Mary his mother, Mary Magdalene, Joanna, and Susanna.[20] Jesus walked alongside these people who became his friends, spending time with them and getting to know and understand them.[21] He shared meals with them and enjoyed their fellowship.[22]

Jesus was especially close to Mary, Martha, and Lazarus—so much so, Scripture tells us that Jesus loved them.[23] What's more insightful is that before Jesus raised Lazarus from the dead, both Mary and Martha said to him, at two different times, "Lord, if you had been here, my brother wouldn't have died."[24]

Can you imagine? They were grieving and heartbroken, but how freeing that they both felt close enough to Jesus to be so honest, to speak their pain, to put it all on the table.[25] And in the midst of all their suffering, they kept trusting Jesus.

What a picture for us of how we can come to Jesus and be just as honest, while at the same time putting our complete trust in him—especially understanding that Jesus is not only our Savior but also our friend. Have you ever thought about that? Have you ever looked to Jesus as your friend? Do you realize that he's called each one of us his friend?

Jesus once said, while explaining our relationship with him,

> No one has greater love than this: to lay down his life for
> his friends. You are my friends if you do what I command

you. I do not call you servants anymore, because a servant doesn't know what his master is doing. I have called you friends, because I have made known to you everything I have heard from my Father. You did not choose me, but I chose you.[26]

Jesus chose us to be his friend. Let that sink in. Though we said yes to Jesus, he chose us before we chose him. If we want our friendship with Jesus to keep flourishing, then we should do with him what we often do with friends—talk, listen, and get to know him. We do this by spending time with Jesus and listening to him as he shares his heart through the Word and by the Spirit. We do it as we share our hearts with him and hear him in prayer. Our friendship with Jesus continues to grow by serving with him to see his mission accomplished in this world.

Over the years, I have observed that people often start strong in their friendship with Jesus, investing time in the relationship and the activities that support it, and then over time move toward self-reliance as they move away from pursuing him in the secret place. But Jesus said to us, "I am the vine; you are the branches. The one who remains in me and I in him produces much fruit, because you can do nothing without me."[27]

There is no friend greater than Jesus and no friendship more precious than his. Yes, we need friends here on earth. We want to be great friends, and we want to seek out great friends, but above all, let's seek to be a great friend of the one who made the greatest sacrifice of all to save us, redeem us, and bring us into friendship with God.

FIND PEOPLE WHO STRENGTHEN YOU

Who are your friends? Who are the people running alongside you, exhorting you to keep moving forward, to stay on mission, and helping you not look back when looking back is all you want to do? Who is it that reminds you what we all need to hear from time to time: "Remember Lot's wife!"? Wouldn't it be great if we all said that to one another every time we began to see each other about to look back, because we know that what often follows looking back is getting stuck—and getting stuck keeps us from moving on with all the plans and purpose God has for us. Every one of us needs life-giving friends who will caution us when we start to drift away from God, even when we don't mean to. We need friends who will speak the truth, even when it's difficult for us to hear.[28] We need true friends who will love us unconditionally and who genuinely want the best for us,[29] who will inspire us and make us better in every way. Scripture tells us, "Iron sharpens iron, and one person sharpens another."[30] What's more, we want to be this same kind of friend, don't we?

We need friends who will encourage us like the writer of Hebrews said.

And let us consider one another in order to provoke love and good works, not neglecting to gather together, as some are in the habit of doing, but encouraging each other, and all the more as you see the day approaching.[31]

We need friends who know how to pray and pray with us, who will help us get into the presence of Jesus when we can't figure out how to get there on our own. There's a story in Mark's gospel that makes this so clear to me. Jesus was speaking in a house full of people, and there was a man outside who was paralyzed and needed to be healed. Because the crowd made it impossible for his four friends to carry him through the front door, they hoisted him up onto the roof, made a hole, and lowered him down into the presence of Jesus. Can you imagine?

They [the friends] came to him [Jesus] bringing a paralytic, carried by four of them. Since they were not able to bring him to Jesus because of the crowd, they removed the roof above him, and after digging through it, they lowered the mat on which the paralytic was lying. Seeing their faith, Jesus told the paralytic, "Son, your sins are forgiven." . . . "I tell you: get up, take your mat, and go home." Immediately he got up, took the mat, and went out in front of everyone. As a result, they were all astounded and gave glory to God, saying, "We have never seen anything like this!"[32]

Can you picture all this happening? The man's friends

had to be strong. They had to be determined. They had to be innovative. When I read this story, I can't help but think of the times in my life when I must have felt like dead weight to my friends. Times when I was stuck and couldn't figure out the way forward on my own. Times when I needed them to carry me. Times when I needed them to pray because I wasn't sure what else to pray.

It would have been the times when I needed godly and faithful friends to tell me what to do because I wasn't sure what next step to take. From my experience, we all need friends who know how to tap into the strength of Jesus and help us. People who are strong enough spiritually to lift us up and carry us when we can't move. People who can get us into the presence of Jesus.

What's more, I can't help but notice what Jesus said when he healed the man: "Seeing their faith . . . Jesus told the paralytic . . . get up, take up your mat, and go home." Jesus saw the faith of the man's friends. Sometimes, we need the faith of our friends to help move us forward in life, to get from the place where we're stuck to where God wants us to go:

- To go from weariness to strength.
- To go from despair to hope.
- To go from chaos to peace.
- To go from the wrong path to the right one.
- To go from confusion to clarity.
- To go from indifference to passion.

- To go from distraction to focus.
- To go from heartache to happiness.
- To go from disappointment to joy.
- To go from "I want to give up" to "I want to go on."
- To go from "I don't know the answer" to "Now I have a plan."

We need our friends to stand with us, to run alongside us, to believe with us as we navigate change, as we step out into new adventures, as we do what we didn't think we were capable of doing. Sometimes, I think our friends know us better than we know ourselves. Maybe that's why, at times, they believe in us more than we believe in ourselves.

WE'RE CREATED FOR COMMUNITY

We were meant to do life together and in community. In her book *Find Your People*, my friend Jennie Allen wrote that "God existed in relationship with himself before any of us were here. It's called the Trinity. God is one, and God is three. . . . For all eternity God has existed in relationship—as Father, Spirit, and Son (Jesus)."[33] This means that God has been relational forever,[34] and since he's created us in his image,[35] he created us out of relationship, for relationship.[36]

Without friends in our lives, we're apt to live in social isolation rather than community—and that's not good. In our post-pandemic world, many of us have gone back to "normal," but there are ways that we might still be steeped in isolation and not be aware of it. I would imagine that we've grown used to working remotely or not hanging out together in person or meeting up for dinner regularly the way we once did. I have worked remotely with many of my team for years because we're spread out around the globe, and I know how isolating it can be. Seeing people on Zoom is great, but building relationships that way can be challenging. Relationships, whether they are with our coworkers or friends, are best built and maintained in person.

I understand we all need and want our own space, and based on our personalities some of us might need solitude more often, but people will most likely be our greatest source of comfort. Following friends on social media can lead us into thinking we're in relationship with them, but if the only place we connect is on social media, then those relationships are virtual, which means they are not real. Our social media account may say we have 500 friends, for example, and we may get all 500 to like a post, but only when we run alongside real people in real life who are running in the same direction that we are can we find genuine friendship. Maybe it's time to reach out to one of those virtual friends and invite them for a cup of coffee.

I understand there's risk involved in such an idea. When we let people come in closer to help us, we run the risk of them hurting us, or us hurting them. We run the risk of being misunderstood, judged wrongly, or betrayed. I've been there, more than once. I know what it's like to be deeply betrayed and want desperately to never let anyone in that close again. If you've been there, then you know that feeling and the pitfalls of swearing off any future hurt. But that's when we need to allow the Holy Spirit to do a healing work in us, and if necessary, seek counseling. We do not want to allow the pain of past relationships to limit the potential of our present and future relationships. We do not want our past bad experiences to control the value God places on friends. We do not want to get stuck in a place of keeping people at arm's length for fear of getting hurt. Instead, we need to process and grieve our loss fully and move on.

> We do not want to allow the pain of past relationships to limit the potential of our present and future relationships.

I have come to understand that some friends are for a season; they are meant to come and go, and that's okay. I've learned that life changes happen, and because of that, there can be a natural unfriending at times. That doesn't necessarily mean we lose a friendship altogether, but it does mean it might shift to a different space in our lives. What's more, as our interests evolve in life, so can our circle of friends. Who all we ran around with early in life, during our school years, or at the beginning of our careers, aren't necessarily the same people we might find ourselves close to years later. Who we work with at one job may become a friend for life, or we may lose touch altogether. As our children age and go through school, we make friends with other parents, but once our kids graduate, it can feel like we graduate too. We recognize that we were brought into each other's lives because our children shared a mutual interest or shared a particular sport, but the friendships we forged weren't meant to be forever.

I've also found that we can have a friend who we think is moving in the same direction as we are, only to suddenly realize that we're moving toward different objectives. It may not be intentional, but differences of opinion we hold dear can begin to move us apart.

Whatever the reasons might be that we lose a friend or two, there are times when we need to find new friends. We don't want to get trapped in a place of "relational stuckness," that place where we're hanging on to friendships that aren't flourishing just because they're friendships we've had for a long time. We want to recognize that new seasons sometimes mean new friends. If that's where you are, begin praying that God will help you find the kind of friend you need, the kind that you just click with.

Ask him to help you find a friend who

- sticks closer than a brother (Proverbs 18:24).
- loves at all times (Proverbs 17:17).
- has godly character (1 Corinthians 15:33).

- forgives easily (Colossians 3:13).
- is tenderhearted (Ephesians 4:32).
- won't judge (James 4:11).
- will help you carry what's heavy (Galatians 6:2).
- will confront and sort through misunderstandings (Colossians 3:12–14).
- is reliable (Proverbs 25:13 MSG; Luke 11:5–8).
- will keep your confidence (Proverbs 16:28; 17:9).
- is wise (Proverbs 13:20).
- will encourage you and build you up (1 Thessalonians 5:11).

In return, do your best to keep growing in Jesus and developing all these same qualities. Be the friend you hope to find, and start there, but don't stop there. Do what's practical to find your new friend. Put yourself out there, be approachable, take some initiative and go places where you're most likely to meet people you'll be compatible with—but not necessarily people who are just like you. God often strengthens us by surrounding us with people who complement us, not people who are just like us. Places to find great friends could include church and all the opportunities to gather that it offers. It could include joining a club, trying out a new gym, volunteering for an organization, taking up a new hobby, or taking a course on something you enjoy. God is a God of abundant grace, and one of the great graces he gives us is that of friends who keep us moving on in the purposes of God.

Remember Lot's Wife ●————————————●

When we read about Lot's wife, we don't read about anyone spurring her on in following God. Imagine the difference that could have made in that moment when she looked back! God wants us to be people who spur each other on!

1. Prayerfully reflect on your friendships. What are strengths you see in your friendships? How can you be a better friend? Are there any friendships you sense God leading you to invest in or distance yourself from?

2. The most important friendship of all is our friendship with Jesus. Take some time to pray and ask, *God, what type of friend am I to you?* Are there any changes that you need to make in the time you spend with him and how you spend that time?

PART THREE

The Rewards of Moving Forward

EIGHT

Arise and Go:
Things Change When We Do

Taking my place at the podium, I paused for a moment, noting that in the audience sat the Mexican secretariat for home affairs, a representative from the United Nations Office on Drugs and Crime, the president of the Citizen Security Council of the Inter-secretarial Commission, and other non-governmental organization (NGO) leaders.

I could not believe this moment was really happening.

I was in Mexico City on behalf of A21 for the launch of *Can You See Me?*—our global media campaign raising awareness about the dangers of human trafficking. Standing there, I couldn't get over the feeling that I was watching a dream come true. I wanted to capture the moment, to hold it close, and to thank God for it, because it was a moment that had been years in the making.

Ever since our team used an iPhone to film our first *Can You See Me?* video, we'd dreamed of a campaign that would reach every continent and every nation where we serve. Through the years it had grown from ideas, experiments, and pilots to a universal message seen on kiosks in airports, as banners on the sides of buses, and on billboards along interstate highways. The campaign stretched to include commercials and short films created to be contextually relevant for a region or nation where we work and to be shown on television in arenas before sports games, in hospitals, shopping malls, corporate offices, spas, restaurants, airports, and on planes. The campaign's printed materials target the most vulnerable in hot spots around the world, where people are being displaced due to war or natural disasters, often landing in refugee camps for days, weeks, months, or years. It truly is an all-out effort to help everyone be a part of the fight against human trafficking. And here we were, launching it not only in Mexico but throughout Latin America.

This surreal moment was largely happening because a young Mexican woman heard me speak about the injustice of human trafficking at a conference in London seven years earlier. Only God could have orchestrated the events of that day that led to this day. Angie, who had her master's degree in data engineering and statistics, came alive when I started sharing the disturbing global human trafficking statistics. For the first time, it occurred to her that this was a very real problem in her own nation, and she could not sit back and pretend that she was not aware. Now that she knew something about human trafficking, she had to do something to help combat it in her own backyard.

Returning home after the conference, she hoped to reach out to A21 in Mexico, only to discover that we didn't have an office or a team there yet. Not letting that deter her interest, she then reached out to our team in California, who gladly helped her. With resources we provided, she began educating herself about human trafficking and in 2014 hosted the first ever Walk for Freedom in Mexico, rallying two hundred people to walk with her. And she didn't stop there.

In 2015, she facilitated six walks in Mexico and Bolivia with hundreds of people walking for freedom. By 2016, there were thirty walks in eight Latin American countries. By 2017, there were forty walks in eleven countries. People were connecting and joining in the fight against human trafficking from Mexico, Guatemala, Colombia, Ecuador, Bolivia, Peru, Argentina, Paraguay, Trinidad and Tobago, Chile, Venezuela, Uruguay, and Brazil.

The number of walks continued to increase as the years marched on, as did the countries hosting walks, and all of this happened because one young woman decided to do something, even when she was not exactly sure what that something would be. What astounds me more than anything is that Angie didn't get stuck looking at everything she could not do, when it would have been perfectly reasonable to do so. Instead, she found the one thing she could do, which led her to the next thing, and then the next thing after that. Because she didn't go back to life as usual when she returned home from London, because she decided to rise up and do what she could with what she had right where she was, in the face of incredible odds, here we were about to launch an anti-trafficking campaign that would literally reach hundreds of millions of people in Latin America. How could I not struggle to take it all in?

DECIDE TO RISE UP

I got through my remarks, and we launched our campaign, but what Angie did has never left me, because it's something we all have to do in our own lives, especially if we want to stop looking back and start moving forward: we have to decide to rise up. We have to be intentional about getting up and moving on in bold faith. Whether we want to make a difference in our own lives, our families, our workplaces, our communities, our churches, or through the work of an organization like A21, we have to rise up right where we are and, using what we can, do what we can. I understand from my own experience that it's easier said than done, but we can't let that deter us.

When I think of all that Angie has forged for the work of A21 in her part of the world, I see a young woman in a long line of women who have risen up over the ages and helped to change the trajectory of one nation or another. There's a particular woman in the Bible whose courage and strength inspires me. In the book of Judges we read about Deborah, a woman who served as a judge in Israel during a time of oppression under the Canaanites. After twenty years of slavery, the Israelites were too beaten down to fight. They needed inspiration. They needed leadership. They needed someone to stand up and take action, and Deborah did.

In Scripture, Deborah said, "Villagers in Israel would not fight, they held back until I, Deborah, arose, until I arose, a mother in Israel."[1] We know from the entire story and this verse that Deborah didn't stay where she was, nor did she let the nation of Israel stay where it was. She arose, mobilized an army, led them into battle, and with her faith in God, she didn't back down. Because of Deborah's courage, the Israelites fought and won. Because she arose, they secured forty years of peace.

Reflecting on her story, I can't escape the reality that one person can affect the destiny of so many others. What's more, it's something we all have the power to do right where we live. In Hebrew, the word *arose* as Deborah used it means "to stand up, to accomplish, to become existent."[2] In the *Merriam-Webster Dictionary*, it is to take action and go from a physical position of sitting down or lying down to standing up.[3] It is a change in posture that can be external or internal, because a change in posture not only describes the bearing of our physical body but also can refer to our attitude or outlook.[4] Think of how many times we have had to arise on the inside and change our attitude mentally, emotionally, and/or spiritually in order to move forward physically. I have no way of knowing what ran through Deborah's mind before she arose, but had I been in her shoes, I would have had to rise up on the inside before I could rise up on the outside. I would have had to change my internal posture before I could change my external posture. I most likely would have gone to the Lord in prayer and quite possibly immersed myself in his promises, especially knowing the enemy I would be facing. I imagine you would have done the same.

Because of this, whether we're speaking about our posture figuratively, spiritually, or physically, it's clear that having the right posture matters and that sometimes we have to purposefully change our posture. So many times when I hear myself telling my girls to sit up straight or to walk with their shoulders back, I sometimes feel like I can hear my mother's voice, because I sound just like she did. "Christina," she would say, "mind your posture. Don't slouch like that. Sit up." Of course, she was speaking about my physical posture, and when she would remind me, I would get so frustrated, because I preferred to slouch. Even when she explained why I needed to sit up straight, I found it so much more comfortable not to. I imagine we all do, because giving in to gravity is always easier than working against it, right? It's more convenient to hunch our shoulders over the table at dinner or to lean over our desks at work. And if you're like me, once I start eating or working, the last thing I'm thinking about is my posture. But alas, Mum was right. She knew the older I grew the more I would care, and she understood that good habits are much easier to form when we're young. So, like Mum, I do my best to keep my girls mindful of their posture—but I have taken it a step further.

Just as much as I've worked to remind our girls about their physical posture, I've done my best to teach them about their spiritual posture—because our spiritual posture is one more thing that affects whether we are living our lives stuck looking back or intentionally moving forward with all the plans and purposes God has for us. If we're slouching, then by definition, we're drooped over; we're moving slowly or reluctantly; we're excessively relaxing our muscles to the point we're assuming an ungainly stooping of the head and shoulders.[5] You could say we're looking down instead of up; that we've grown passive and laid-back when God wants us on the edge of what he's doing and moving forward with him. Could it be that Lot's wife was slouching in some way? She certainly wasn't running for the hills with gusto, because she stopped and looked back—and then she got stuck looking back for eternity. And none of us want that.

It's so easy, especially after the past few years of our world changing faster than we can keep up with and dealing

> Our spiritual posture is one more thing that affects whether we are living our lives stuck looking back or intentionally moving forward with all the plans and purposes God has for us.

with all that the pandemic has thrown at us, to stop caring as much about our posture. To start slouching, spiritually speaking. To start moving slowly or reluctantly. To forget that we're in a spiritual battle, fighting against powers and principalities, with a mission to fulfill and purpose to outwork.[6] To forget to put on our spiritual armor.[7] To forget that we're fighting the good fight of faith.[8] To stop looking up. To stop getting up. To stop moving forward. To start growing lazy. To not want to go to church, read the Bible, pray, serve others, or even put on real pants. You might be laughing at such a thought, but let's face it, we've worn "stay-at-home" clothes for a few years now. Even when we Zoom, I'm not sure our bottom halves look as polished as our top halves. We've seen all the memes and heard all the jokes about it, but it's real. There are so many things we took far more seriously before the pandemic changed our world, including wearing real pants. I suppose many of the things we've let go will never matter, but the condition of our spiritual posture will always matter.

I understand there are times when looking back is easier than looking up. That giving up is easier than getting up. That standing down is easier than standing up. Especially when we've been beaten down, knocked down, ridiculed, canceled, maligned, misunderstood, abandoned, or rejected, when everything seems hopeless and we feel helpless. When we're afraid and feel paralyzed. When we've grown indifferent and apathetic, though we never meant for that to happen.

Still, if we've let our spiritual posture go by the wayside the same way we have become careless in getting dressed for the day, then perhaps we need to ask ourselves:

- Are we looking up? "Let us run with endurance the race that lies before us, keeping our eyes on Jesus, the pioneer and perfecter of our faith."[9]
- Are we getting up? "Get up, sleeper, and rise up from the dead, and Christ will shine on you."[10]
- Are we standing up? "For this reason take up the full armor of God, so that you may be able to resist in the evil day, and having prepared everything, to take your stand."[11]

We would do well to come back to these questions frequently, as I have found that we tend to slouch spiritually over time without even realizing it. Typically our slouching goes unnoticed by us because we've become comfortable in it and accustomed to it, which means that unless we are paying careful attention to our posture—or unless someone brings it to our attention—we overlook it.

CHANGE YOUR POSTURE

Where in your life have you grown comfortable and started slouching? And overlooking it? It's so easy to give in to the gravitational pull of ease and let slouching creep into every area of our lives, but wherever we find it, that's where we need to change our posture; that's where we need to rise up. I can't help but wonder if this is how Lot's wife slowly became someone who would stop and look back instead of obeying and running for her future.

In my life, when I don't want to do something, I can feel myself starting to slouch, figuratively speaking. I find that rising up requires vigilance and intentionality not only spiritually but also physically, mentally, and relationally. When I travel, for example, I go to the gym as soon as I can after landing. On a recent trip to Cambodia, Thailand, and Pakistan, my body was weary when I landed in each country, and the last thing I wanted to do was hit the gym, but I did it anyway to combat jet lag. I would have rather slept, and while sleep is important, so is exercise. I've learned that to fight jet lag, it's best to do the opposite of what I feel, so I hit the gym first. It's part of how I keep myself from slouching physically, and it keeps me awake and alert to fulfill the purpose for which I have traveled to those nations. No matter where I am, I try to exercise every day, so I hike and bike; I walk, lift weights, and run. I've learned to not let myself think about it or I might not ever exercise. It would be much easier to give in to my aching joints, particularly as I age, but I can't.

I understand that for some of us, such exercise might be difficult. Some of us have suffered injuries, setbacks, illnesses, or even diseases that have left us with limitations or changed realities. But where it's possible, let's keep moving physically. Let's care for our bodies as the temples of God that they are.[12] Let's eat healthy instead of thinking we'll get around to it later. Let's ask God to strengthen us to steward the gift and grace of life he has entrusted to us. If we think we're short on time to work good habits into our routines, then let's ask God how we can make the most of our time.

When I find myself slouching mentally, I step up and redirect my thought life. If you have read any of my books, then you know that I have worked very hard to renew my mind so that my thinking is in alignment with the truth of the Word of God and not my own feelings or ideas.[13] This is something I have continued to do every single day of my life. Our minds are truly a battlefield and if we're not diligent, our thoughts will always spiral into fear, doubt, negativity, indifference, and apathy. We'll naturally tend to ruminate rather than renew, so we have to intentionally dwell on what God commands us to think about: "Whatever is true, whatever is honorable, whatever is just, whatever is pure, whatever is lovely, whatever is commendable—if there is any moral excellence and if there is anything praiseworthy—dwell on these things."[14]

What this verse makes clear is that we are to purposefully direct our thoughts—and not be directed by our thoughts. Does what you think about draw you closer to God and result in you having greater love for and confidence in God? Or does what you think about lead you into negativity, disbelief, doubt, despair, and anxiety? When we find ourselves defaulting to the latter, then we need to change our posture.

When I catch myself slouching relationally, I begin reprioritizing my time with Nick, my girls, my team, and my friends, because this kind of slouching happens when we stop investing in and pursuing others, either out of fatigue, misplaced priorities, disappointment, hurt, betrayal, or for some other reason. I know that when I'm weary, my tendency is to pull back from my friendships, to get lazy in my marriage and mothering, and to just lie in a hammock, but I can't let myself do that.

If you're married, then maybe, for you, slouching looks more like drifting from dates and time spent together. Maybe it looks like sporadic, factual check-ins and binging television series, or being in proximity without being present.

With our kids, slouching can happen when we grow more invested in their performance than their discipleship, when we grow more invested in providing for them than connecting with them. It can happen when we become more consumed with what we need to get done than with taking the time to ask our kids about their friends, school, sports, and interests.

In our friendships, slouching can happen when we stop following up and following through, when we stop asking and answering, when we stop reaching out and responding. It can also look like going it alone, refusing to build again, trust again, try again, because of what has been before.

And in our church communities, slouching can happen when we stop showing up or when we come but don't contribute, focusing solely on what we can get rather than what we can give to everyone else.

To stop slouching in any area requires a change in posture, and a change in posture means we don't stay where we once were and we don't do what we once did. Hiking has taught me so much about this. When I reach the summit of a mountain, not only do I experience a feeling of accomplishment and a renewed sense of strength, but the view always amazes me. From the tops of mountains, I've seen the ocean, I've seen other peaks I've climbed, I've seen cities nestled in valleys, and I've taken in vast forests. There's nothing else that compares, and as much as I always want to linger there, to sit there and keep taking it all in, I have to move on. I have to get up and head back down the mountain before nightfall.

The transition of reaching the top, feeling stunned by the view, sitting down to rest, taking it all in, and then getting back up and trekking on has taught me something about other areas of my life: In the moments when we are enjoying the most comfortable of circumstances, it seems far easier to hesitate and stay seated. It seems far easier to give in to where we are rather than stand up and get going in the direction God is leading us. But that will never be God's plan for us; his plan will always include changing our posture and moving on in bold faith.

RISING UP FROM COMFORT AND EASE

It is often easier to maintain the status quo, to stay comfortable and not exert the pressure required to change our posture.

That is often why we do not rise up. We are surrounded by luxuries and conveniences that make our lives comfortable. From having refrigerators and microwaves, TV remotes and garage door openers, electric blankets and seat warmers, phones and laptops, we're used to life being made easier than ever. When I travel and don't have access to the comforts I'm accustomed to, I realize how comfortable I have become. I can order books, household items, and new gym shorts from Amazon, and they will deliver them to my home, sometimes the same day. I can order a meal from my favorite restaurant and DoorDash will bring it to my door. I have my choice of numerous streaming services I can watch in my air-conditioned home, while I sit on my nice, comfy couch. I can take a hot shower most any time I want, unless my girls have taken a shower recently and used up all the hot water. But even then, it's not long until we have hot water again. Do we even realize how many conveniences shape our everyday lives? I wonder whether the potential loss of such comfort and ease is another reason that we need to remember Lot's wife.

We know that Sodom was very fruitful before it was destroyed—so much so, it was compared to the garden of Eden—a region with all kinds of food that was a blessing.[15] It was the mercy and goodness of God that everyone who lived there had such abundance, but the people were taking all of it for granted: "Now this was the sin of your sister Sodom: She and her daughters were arrogant, overfed and unconcerned; they did not help the poor and needy. They were haughty and did detestable things before me. Therefore I did away with them as you have seen."[16]

That is one of those verses that I think is worth reading and rereading until it does its full work in our souls. The people in Sodom prized and idolized their comfort. They were blessed, greatly blessed, but instead of being a river of blessing, releasing what they received for the benefit of others, they became a reservoir of blessing, retaining what they received for the benefit of themselves—and the truth is that Sodom is not that far away from where we are today. Spiritually, many of us have purchased real estate in Sodom and have grown accustomed to its culture. We, too, can be arrogant. We, too, can be overfed and unconcerned. We, too, can turn a blind eye to the poor and needy. Living that way is so commonplace today, I believe we will find ourselves adrift in the current of Sodom's self-centeredness unless we prayerfully and intentionally choose to do otherwise.

What does it look like to choose otherwise? God doesn't leave us guessing. Over and over again in Scripture, God shows what he wants us to do with what we receive from him. In 2 Corinthians, Paul was comforted by God, and even with comfort—not just tangible resources—he understood that what God has given is not to be pooled but to be passed on.

Blessed be the God and Father of our Lord Jesus Christ, the Father of mercies and the God of all comfort. He comforts us in all our affliction, so that we may be able to comfort those who are in any kind of affliction, through the comfort we ourselves receive from God. For just as the sufferings of Christ overflow to us, so also through Christ our comfort overflows. If we are afflicted, it is for your comfort and salvation. If we are comforted, it is for your comfort, which produces in you patient endurance of the same sufferings that we suffer.[17]

The comfort God gave was God's provision for Paul, but it was not God's provision only for Paul. What was received from God was intended to be released, not retained, to bless and benefit others. God wants this to be what we do with all we receive from him, and the number one thing that will hold us back from doing that is concern with our own comfort. It's concern for our own comfort that will lead us to withhold, fearing that if we give, we might not have. It's concern for our own comfort that will keep us from risking, esteeming the cost to us, imagined or actual, as greater than the benefit to the other. It's concern for our comfort that will lead us to take up residency in complacency's zip code and fail to live for the purposes of God and respond to the pleas around us. Simply, concern for our comfort will lead us to repeat the sins of Sodom and make us want to stay right where we are.

It's so easy to sit down, to become apathetic and indifferent, concerned with our comfort, and not get back up. But that is not the call of God on our lives, and it has never been the call of God on any of his people's lives. All throughout Scripture, God repeatedly calls his people to arise—even when they are downcast, even when they are fearful, even when they are unsure of what to do next, even when arising will cost them their safety, their security, and their comfort:

- When God wanted to free the children of Israel from the Egyptians, God told Moses to arise.[18]
- When God wanted the nation of Israel to cross the Jordan River into the promised land, God told Joshua to arise.[19]
- When the Midianites were oppressing Israel, God called on Gideon to arise.[20]
- When God wanted David anointed as the next king of Israel, God told Samuel to arise.[21]
- When there was a drought in the land, and Elijah needed to be fed, God called on the widow of Zarephath to arise.[22]
- When God's people were far from him spiritually and only growing in distance, God called Jeremiah to arise.[23]
- When there was an edict of genocide for the Jews, God led Esther to arise.[24]
- When the temple needed to be rebuilt, God called Nehemiah to arise.[25]

In the New Testament, when Jesus healed people, he often told them to arise:

- To Jairus's daughter, he said, "Talitha koum!" which is translated, "Little girl, I say to you, get up."[26]

- To the young man whose funeral was underway, Jesus said, "Young man, I say to you, arise. . . ."[27]
- To the man with the withered hand, Jesus said, "Get up and come forward!"[28]
- To the paralytic, Jesus said, "Get up! Pick up your mat and walk."[29]

And when the Jews began persecuting him for healing the paralytic, Jesus said, "My Father is still working, and I am working also."[30] Jesus said this because God was still working then, and I feel sure he is still working now. Because all is not yet fulfilled. Because all is not as he intended it to be. And it won't be until there is a new heaven and a new earth, but that doesn't mean there isn't much that he wants to be accomplishing while we're living in the here and now. There are still so many people who have not seen, who do not know, and have not heard that God loves them, that God wants to save, rescue, and redeem them. I feel sure you know some of them.

Rising up, especially rising up again, is not always easy—especially when we are tired, especially when we are winded, especially when we've been wounded. Comfort is, well, comfortable, and rising up is not. But the good news is that our ability to arise is not based on our strength but on the one who

- never grows faint or weary (Isaiah 40:28);
- renews our strength as we wait on him (Isaiah 40:31);
- is greater than he who is in the world (1 John 4:4);

- is strong when we are weak (2 Corinthians 12:10);
- is all strength (Psalm 147:5);
- makes us strong in the strength of his might (Ephesians 6:10);
- has promised us that he will never leave us nor forsake us (Hebrews 13:5).

I understand that it's so easy to inadvertently sit back and wait for circumstances to change before we arise, to wait for the people in our lives to change, to wait for our workplaces to change, to wait for the government to change, but God has given us more agency than that. He's placed inside us the same power that raised Jesus from the dead. "And if the Spirit of him who raised Jesus from the dead lives in you, then he who raised Christ from the dead will also bring your mortal bodies to life through his Spirit who lives in you."[31]

Because Jesus arose, we can arise. Because of Jesus, we can be the most hope-filled, faith-filled, joy-filled people on the planet. We can have more clarity, purpose, determination, strength, and endurance than anyone. We can be full of wisdom, creativity, vision, ideas, and projects. I know our world has changed. I said as much at the very beginning of this book, and all throughout this book, but Jesus has not changed. His promises have

> Because of Jesus, we can be the most hope-filled, faith-filled, joy-filled people on the planet.

not changed. His plans for us have not changed. His purpose for us has not changed. That's why, more than ever, it is time for us to arise. It's time for us to move on in bold faith, but that doesn't happen automatically. We have to rise up and do something with what we have right where we are, and we have to do it over and over each and every day.

Every morning when you wake up, I encourage you to have a conversation with the Lord and ask:

- *God, what is on your heart today and how do you want me to arise and participate in what you want to do?*
- *God, what stronghold do you want demolished in the place of prayer today?*
- *What need do you want to meet through me today?*
- *What hope do you want to extend through me today?*
- *What wrong do you want to right through me today?*
- *What injustice do you want to cease through me today?*
- *What suffering do you want to end through me today?*
- *What pain do you want to comfort through me today?*
- *What words of life do you want spoken through me today?*

Ask with your family, your friends, your coworkers, your neighbors, your community, and beyond in mind. Ask God boldly and anticipate his answer, and then act in accordance with what he says.

So often we frame things as though we are waiting for

God, but what if God is waiting for us? To ask and to act on his answer? Let's never forget what he has said to us and about us: "For we are his workmanship, created in Christ Jesus for good works, which God prepared ahead of time for us to do."[32] The great good that God wants to do—and the great good that God wants to do through each of us—is not an afterthought but a forethought of God. How incredible is that? Knowing that, let's not turn his forethought into our afterthought. Let's awake, let's ask, let's anticipate, and let's arise to act on his answer, for his praise and his purpose! There's no telling what God can do through us as we arise and obey.

Remember Lot's Wife

Lot's wife's doubt, disobedience, and lack of fearing God were signs of spiritual slouching.

1. Take some time to pray: *God, are there areas where I am slouching—physically, relationally, or even spiritually—and if so, how do I need to change my posture?* Record your insights and next steps in your journal.

2. God is calling us to rise up and join him in his purposes on this planet. As you think about your family, friends, neighbors, coworkers, and community, what is God calling you to rise up and address? What is one step you can take to do that today?

CONCLUSION

Go With Your Eyes Toward Home

Dropping my carry-on bag on the floor of our bedroom, I couldn't wait to change clothes and crawl under the covers of my very own bed. Nick and I had just arrived home after traveling for fourteen weeks to our global A21 offices in twelve countries, and though I had slept well in most every bed in every city, there's not a bed in this world that sleeps like my own. I'm not entirely sure why, but I'm somehow convinced that my bed knows all my aches and pains, the old and the new, and adjusts accordingly. It knows how to hold me just right for six to eight hours at a time. I think it even knows when I need to be woken up a bit to turn over, as though it monitors me all through the night. I promise that I'm not in a delirium from jet lag—or maybe I am—but I genuinely love sleeping in my bed above all others, and when I come home from a long trip, I can't wait to jump into bed and get a good night's sleep.

If you travel, then maybe you know the feeling. I imagine that it probably doesn't have much to do with the brand of mattress either of us sleep on but more with the fact that our beds are covered in our sheets and our blankets and topped with our pillows. I would think it has to do with how it smells, how it feels, and how we might relax in our own beds more than any other. Most of all, I suppose it has to do with the fact that we're home.

Wherever we live around the globe, wherever we call home, being home is a feeling like no other, isn't it? Most of my happiest memories revolve around being home with Nick and our girls, celebrating a holiday, cooking in the kitchen, eating dinner together, or curling up on the sofa in front of a warm, cozy fire. Still, traveling as much as I do, taking laps around the globe, I've been asked many times where it is that I feel most at home, particularly since I was born and raised in Sydney and now live in the United States.

It's a fair question, especially since I've joked through the years that I live on a plane. I'll admit that when Nick and I and our girls go to Sydney for a visit, even before I land—while looking out my airplane window and seeing the iconic Sydney Harbor Bridge—I feel a sense of home. When I walk through customs and see the sign that says "Welcome home," I feel it. When I sit at a café and eat Vegemite toast, I feel a sense of home. When I visit familiar streets and sites, I feel a sense of home. When I connect with old friends and laugh about old memories, I feel a sense of home. But having a sense of home is different from being home, so I actually don't consider Sydney my home.

There have been times when I've spent months looking forward to visiting a familiar restaurant or park or shoreline while we're there, only to find when I get there that it's not the same. It looks the same but it's not the same. And I think it's because I've changed. I've moved on in my life, so when I go back for a visit, it's really not the home I left.

Likewise, now that I have lived in the United States for more than a decade, I often experience the same feelings. When I look out my airplane window and catch the familiar views of the coast of Southern California, I feel a sense of home. It happens when I turn into our neighborhood, when I meet with friends at my favorite restaurant, when I go to the gym, or when I head into our California office. But again, having a sense of home is different from actually being home, so despite living in the US for more than a decade, I'm not sure I consider it my home either.

Before you think I travel too much and need to stay put for a while to sort all this out, what I really know is that as followers of Christ, wherever we might live in this world, wherever we may feel a sense of home, that place is not our home, because our home isn't anywhere here on earth. Even if you happen to be one of those people who gets to live in the same town where generations of your family have lived, our real home has an eternal address with a heavenly zip code. The writer of Hebrews put it this way: "For this world is not our permanent home; we are looking forward to a home yet to come."[1] Perhaps that's why, at the core of my being, nowhere really feels like home to me, not even the place where I crawl into my favorite bed.

Because this world is not my eternal home any more than it is yours, we are what the Bible calls *sojourners*, meaning we are people who are passing through this life as we head toward home. It was Peter who used this term when he wrote to the persecuted Christians who had been dispersed throughout five regions of Asia Minor.

> Beloved, I urge you as sojourners and exiles to abstain from the passions of the flesh, which wage war against your soul. Keep your conduct among the Gentiles honorable, so that when they speak against you as evildoers, they may see your good deeds and glorify God on the day of visitation.[2]

Because we're sojourners, we cannot let ourselves get stuck anywhere along the way—wherever that might be—spiritually, mentally, emotionally, relationally, or physically. We were never meant to stop and stay but to keep moving forward. That's why it's so important to remember Lot's wife in our day-to-day lives, so we keep ourselves moving forward toward our eventual home.

In the Hebrew and Greek, a sojourner is defined as "a foreigner who is traveling through a land or one who has taken up residence in that land. The sojourner has no familial or tribal affiliation with those among whom he or she is traveling or living."[3] There are many sojourners throughout the Bible, but one of the first that comes to mind is Abraham.

> By faith Abraham, when called to go to a place he would later receive as his inheritance, obeyed and went, without knowing where he was going. By faith he sojourned in the land of the promise, as in a foreign country, having dwelt in tents with Isaac and Jacob, the joint-heirs of the same promise.[4]

I recognize that *sojourner* is not a word we use in our everyday conversations, and yet, based on these definitions, it could easily apply to myriad situations. When I travel, I'm a sojourner, whether I'm visiting a city within the US or one in Europe, Australasia, the Middle East, South America, Africa, or Southeast Asia. When Catherine went to college for her freshman year, a couple of hours away from home, she was a sojourner there. When volunteers for A21 move to be near one of our offices for a three-to-six-month internship, they are sojourners in whatever city they are serving. In each of these scenarios, we are all people who are passing through a particular place for a season of time; we're not people who are stopping and staying because we've reached a permanent place. And yet, while we're in the temporary place, we're fully present and engaged in the moment, but again, we know that it isn't a forever assignment. We will eventually move on to some other place—because that's what sojourners do.

LIVING AS SOJOURNERS *HERE* AND CITIZENS *THERE*

When I first came to America in 1998, I was naturally a citizen of Australia, so I had to come on a visitor visa. It was understood that I was coming to visit and that my time in the United States would be temporary, and at some point, I would have to leave. In a sense, I was a sojourner, because I was passing through and not staying. What's more, while I was afforded the same protection given to a citizen, I didn't have the same rights and responsibilities of a citizen. Whether or not I got to enter the country, for example, was determined by the US Customs and Border Protection immigration inspectors. If I was allowed into the country, I couldn't overstay any longer than 180 days, otherwise I could be barred from reentry for three years. If I overstayed a year or more, then I could be barred from reentry for ten years.[5]

For twelve years, I traveled to the US this way, but in 2010, I moved to the US and became what the US government called a *resident alien*. Being a resident alien meant I was an immigrant living in the US, and as such, I had the right to obtain a social security number and work in the US, though I did not have the right to vote. I also had responsibilities to fulfill to keep this new status, otherwise I could be deported. I had to file income taxes and obey all the laws of the US, states, and localities. I had to support the democratic form of government and notify the US Department of Citizenship and Immigration Services of any address changes.[6]

In March 2012, my status changed to a permanent resident alien. With this promotion, I could now do everything I could do before, but I was considered permanent—an important distinction that put me closer to obtaining citizenship.

In July 2018, I passed my citizenship test, eight years to the day that we moved to America. When Nick and I, and our girls, took the Naturalization Oath of Allegiance to the United States of America on September 18, 2018, it was a memorable day. I finally became a citizen of the United States of America. This meant I could now register to vote in state and federal elections. I could serve on a jury. I could have access to federal benefits. I could travel with a US passport and be protected by the US government while in another country. I could reenter the US freely. I could be eligible for federal jobs and run for public office. As a naturalized citizen I now had all the rights and privileges of a citizen born in the US.[7]

I know I've just given you an abbreviated version of my path to citizenship in the US, but I did that to make the point that it was not until I became a citizen that I had full rights and privileges. In the same way, no matter where on earth you are reading this book, and what country is on the front of your passport, if you are in Christ, then you are actually a citizen of heaven and a resident of earth. You have rights and privileges that come from another realm. When Paul wrote to the Philippians, he said, "We, however, are citizens of heaven, and we eagerly wait for our Savior, the Lord Jesus Christ, to come from heaven. He will change our weak mortal bodies and make them like his own glorious body, using that power by which he is able to bring all things under his rule."[8]

By calling the Philippians "citizens of heaven," Paul was painting a metaphor for the Philippians and for us. We live temporarily in a colony called Earth, but we are citizens of heaven, and as citizens of heaven, we have rights and privileges as well as assignments and responsibilities, just like we do as the citizens of any nation here on earth.

SOJOURNING WITH PURPOSE

As citizens of heaven and sojourners on this earth, one of the responsibilities we have as we live *here* is to live for *there*. To pursue things *here* that matter *there*. To do things *here* that matter *there*. To be about the things *here* that matter *there*.

It is so important for us to understand that life as a sojourner is not one of aimlessness but purposefulness. When we, as

> As citizens of heaven and sojourners on this earth, one of the responsibilities we have as we live *here* is to live for *there*.

sojourners, lose sight of our purpose, we become either settlers or squanderers. Settlers are those who settle down as they become satisfied and satiated with this life; they stop moving and stop pursuing the purposes of God, as the Israelites did once they entered the promised land, never taking all of it.[9] Squanderers are those who wander and waste what has been given by God, swapping it for a lesser and lower purpose, as the Israelites did in the wilderness. But settling is not the call of God on our lives and squandering is not the call of God on our lives. We are called by God to live as sojourners, a people on the move who are in pursuit of God and his purposes.

What does it look like to live as a sojourner with purpose? There is no better example than Jesus Christ. While he sojourned here, he had his eyes fixed on one thing and one thing only: doing the will and the work of the Father.[10] This singular focus was so great that it directed what he said and didn't say and what he did and didn't do.[11] As a sojourner, Jesus lived a life of purpose.

There's a Greek word used throughout the New Testament, *telos*, that speaks to this reality. I'm about to give you a quick Greek lesson, so please stay with me. I promise this is going to be good. Used as a noun, telos essentially means "end goal or ultimate purpose." As an adjective, it can mean "finished, lacking nothing necessary to completeness, perfect." As a verb, it can mean "to bring to an end, to complete, to perfect."[12] Jesus used this word several times to describe what he did, what he pursued, while on this earth.

John 4:34: "My food is to do the will of him who sent me and to finish [*teleioó*] his work."

John 5:36: "But I have a greater testimony than John's because of the works that the Father has given me to accomplish [teleioó]. These very works I am doing testify about me that the Father has sent me."

John 17:4: "I have glorified you on the earth by completing [teleioó] the work you gave me to do."

Jesus' telos was to teleioó the work of God, or in other words, Jesus' goal was to complete the work of God that he had for him. As those who are in Christ, we have the same call: to serve the purposes of God in our generation, as David did.[13]

So what are God's purposes and plans? What is the end he is working toward? God has a grand telos for the whole world. He's going to restore everything to how he intended it to be. He is in the midst of reconciling it all back to himself in Christ. There is redemption going on, and all things will be made right. God will be glorified. That's his telos.[14]

As those who belong to God, our *telos* is found in his *telos*. Paul captured this truth when he wrote, "But I consider my life of no value to myself; my purpose is to finish [teleioó] my course and the ministry I received from the Lord Jesus, to testify to the gospel of God's grace."[15]

God's telos, and the pursuit of it, keeps us from settling and it keeps us from squandering. It keeps us moving forward on purpose as sojourners of purpose. God's telos is why we must remember Lot's wife.

FULFILLING OUR *TELOS*

So as sojourners who are residents of earth and as citizens of heaven, how practically do we live in line with God's telos? We are told: "Therefore, we are ambassadors for Christ, since God is making his appeal through us. We plead on Christ's behalf, 'Be reconciled to God.'"[16]

On the world stage, an ambassador is someone who lives in one country while representing their home country. In the United States they are the

president's highest-ranking representative to a specific nation or international organization abroad. An effective ambassador has to be a strong leader—a good manager, a resilient negotiator, and a respected representative of the United States. A key role of an ambassador is to coordinate the activities not only of the Foreign Service Officers and staff serving under him, but also representatives of other U.S. agencies in the country.[17]

Most every nation on earth has ambassadors serving around the world. Because of the work of A21, we have relationships with ambassadors around the globe, particularly in the nations where we have offices. In much the same way, you and I have been sent by God into this world to represent Christ our King:[18]

- As an ambassador, we speak the message of God who sends us (1 Corinthians 15:1–4).
- As an ambassador, we speak with the authority of God who sends us (Matthew 28:18–20).

- As an ambassador, we are in constant communication with God who sends us (1 Thessalonians 5:17).
- As an ambassador, we can bring heaven to earth as we pray and obey (Matthew 6:10).
- As an ambassador, we can bring the love of heaven into a world filled with hate.
- As an ambassador, we can bring the steadfast joy of the Spirit into a world of uncertainty.
- As an ambassador, we can bring the peace of God into a world that is gripped by anxiety.
- As an ambassador, we can bring the patience of God in a world dominated by instant gratification.
- As an ambassador, we can bring kindness, goodness, faithfulness, gentleness, and self-control of the Spirit of God to a world that is so often starved of these things.
- As an ambassador, we can bring the hope of God to a world that is hurting.
- As an ambassador, we can bring the comfort of God to hearts that are suffering.

As an ambassador filled by the Spirit of God, we can be used by God to help bring heaven to earth, which means it won't get done if we don't do it. We are the ones called to bring heaven to earth in our workplaces, in our homes, and in our communities. We are afforded privileges. Therefore, we must live our lives on earth in such a way that we represent the

values of our heavenly home and point others toward this ultimate end. We live here, work here, build here, and serve here,
but we are not staying here; we are on our way home. Knowing
this does not make us abdicate our responsibilities here; in
fact, it ought to propel us to want to be immensely fruitful
here, knowing we will give an account for all we have done
here when we get there.

WHEN WE'RE FINALLY HOME

The longer I live, and the closer to death I get, the more I realize people are very uncomfortable talking about going home to
heaven—even though we surely all agree that's where we want
to go when this life is over. I've even found that some people are
afraid of death, though Scripture promises us that because of
Jesus' death, burial, and resurrection, death has lost its sting.[19]
It has no power over us. Still, it's not something most people
want to talk about at the next dinner party. I've lost so many
people in the past decade of my life, because that's what happens
as you age—we lose our parents, we lose our aunts and uncles,
we lose other family members, and we lose our friends. What I
didn't expect as I aged was to live through a pandemic and lose
even more family and friends, something we've all experienced
together. All this loss in recent years has made me think more
about going home than any other time in my life. It's made me
more curious about heaven and what it will really be like.

When I was a child, and people would talk of heaven, I would sometimes imagine the angels I'd seen depicted in the stained glass windows at our church, because in my family, everyone often spoke of angels when someone died. I'd hear them say things like God needed another angel in heaven, or the angels came and escorted the "dearly departed," or God must have needed another travel agent in heaven, because that was the occupation of the deceased here on earth. I was never quite sure what any of those statements meant, or why God would need a travel agent—after all, he's God and is supposed to already be everywhere.[20] But I deduced from what I saw at church that angels played some important role and must come in a variety of sizes for one reason or another.

Although I don't know what heaven will be like, I know we won't be sitting around bored playing harps, because there will be work to do. The book of Revelation tells us that we will rest from our labor here on earth,[21] but as God's servants in heaven, we will spend our time there serving him.[22] We will build, plant, and enjoy the work of our hands.[23]

I'm not sure what all my options will be when I get there, but I'm totally down for joining the cloud of witnesses leaning over the balcony of heaven that the writer of Hebrews mentioned.[24] I want to cheer everyone on who is still here. There certainly won't be any need for the evangelist that I've spent a lifetime being, because clearly everyone in heaven will have been saved. Come to think of it, I'm pretty certain that a number of jobs will be completely unnecessary. There won't be a need for funeral services, for sure, because there is no death in heaven. There won't be any need for doctors and nurses, or paramedics and EMTs, or any other medical services or pharmaceuticals, because no one will be sick. Come to think of it, I don't think we'll need any tissues either, because there will be no more tears.[25] There won't be any need for arms manufacturers, because there won't be any war.[26] There won't be any need for hair stylists or nail techs or personal trainers because our bodies will be glorified.[27] There won't be any need for politicians, or law enforcement, or insurance salesmen, or bankers, or divorce lawyers, because no one will need their services.[28] I don't mean to threaten everyone's careers, but in heaven, we might have to attend a job fair and start over.

In all seriousness, sometimes I think we don't talk about our eternal home and the fact that we're headed home because we think it's an end that's scary or mythical or morbid. But it's not an end; it's a continuation, and one that Scripture describes beautifully. Not only will we not have to work and toil the way we have to here on earth, but we'll get to enjoy all the benefits of our eternal home:

- **There will be his presence:** "Then I heard a loud voice from the throne: Look, God's dwelling is with humanity, and he will live with them. They will be his peoples, and God himself will be with them and will be their God."[29]
- **There will be worship:** "After this I looked, and there was a vast multitude from every nation, tribe, people, and

language, which no one could number, standing before the throne and before the Lamb. They were clothed in white robes with palm branches in their hands. And they cried out in a loud voice: Salvation belongs to our God, who is seated on the throne, and to the Lamb!"[30]

- **There will be light:** "Night will be no more; people will not need the light of a lamp or the light of the sun, because the Lord God will give them light, and they will reign forever and ever."[31]

- **There will be life:** "The world and its desires pass away, but whoever does the will of God will live forever."[32]

- **There will be mansions:** "In my Father's house are many rooms. If it were not so, would I have told you that I am going to prepare a place for you? If I go away and prepare a place for you, I will come again and take you to myself, so that where I am you may be also."[33]

- **There will be blessing:** "Then he showed me the river of the water of life, clear as crystal, flowing from the throne of God and of the Lamb down the middle of the city's main street. The tree of life was on each side of the river, bearing twelve kinds of fruit, producing its fruit every month. The leaves of the tree are for healing the nations, and there will no longer be any curse."[34]

- **There will be peace and joy:** "For this reason they are before the throne of God, and they serve him day and night in his temple. The one seated on the throne will shelter them: They will no longer hunger; they will no longer thirst; the sun will no longer strike them, nor will any scorching heat. For the Lamb who is at the center of the throne will shepherd them; he will guide them to springs of the waters of life, and God will wipe away every tear from their eyes."[35]

- **There will be beauty:** "The building material of its wall was jasper, and the city was pure gold clear as glass. The foundations of the city wall were adorned with every kind of jewel: the first foundation is jasper, the second sapphire, the third chalcedony, the fourth emerald, the fifth sardonyx, the sixth carnelian, the seventh chrysolite, the eighth beryl, the ninth topaz, the tenth chrysoprase, the eleventh jacinth, the twelfth amethyst. The twelve gates are twelve pearls; each individual gate was made of a single pearl. The main street of the city was pure gold, transparent as glass."[36]

When we get home, there will be no more battles. Every bondage we fought so hard to overcome will be no more. The pain, the suffering, the addiction, the fatigue, the worry, the disappointment, the stress, the eight-to-five will all be gone. We'll be in the presence of Jesus, and everything will be perfect.[37] I imagine if we look back at our life here on earth, we'll be so glad God made us sojourners. We'll be so glad he made us ambassadors *here* and citizens *there*. We'll be so glad that we're finally home.

Knowing what awaits me in my eternal home is what keeps

me going here on earth. Knowing that my efforts here will have an eternal reward there keeps me pressing on, running my race, reaching for the prize here, which is Jesus.[38] We all face disappointment, pain, suffering, sickness, disease, loss, trials, temptations, heartbreak, grief, and betrayal, because we live in a fallen world. I, like you, must choose daily to remember who I am, why I'm here, and where I am going, so I don't keep looking back and getting stuck in these places. I, too, must take the words of Jesus seriously and remember Lot's wife.

> Knowing what awaits me in my eternal home is what keeps me going here on earth.

It's not easy to keep moving forward, but knowing that the same power that raised Jesus from the dead lives in us makes it possible no matter what we face here on earth.[39] We don't have to stop; we don't have to quit; we don't have to get stuck. I know the world has changed, but our God does not change.[40] I know life can often disappoint us, but God is always faithful.[41] I know that obstacles can seem daunting, but greater is he that is in us than he who is in the world.[42] I know we are surrounded by darkness, but our God is light, and in him there is no darkness.[43] I know it might look impossible, but with God all things are possible.[44] I know it often feels lonely, but God promises to never leave nor forsake us.[45] I know we can feel weak, but that is when his strength is made perfect in us.[46] God has placed us on this planet, in this period of time, to bear much fruit, to bring him great glory.[47] He has empowered us with Holy Spirit so that we can run our race and finish our course for his praise.

Friends, I am convinced that if Lot's wife would have responded to her moment of decision through the eyes of eternity, she would have chosen differently. Let's be those who remember Lot's wife; let's be those who choose differently. As we run the race of this life and complete the course God has given us, let's keep our eyes fixed squarely ahead on Jesus Christ, the author and perfecter of our faith.[48] Let's be those who run forward in hope and with hope, with our eyes fixed on God and the good he has ahead, because we are those who remember that while the world changes, God does not. Let's be those who run forward, with our eyes fixed on God and the good he has ahead, because we trust God and his goodness, because we know we are sent and commissioned by the King of heaven, because he gives us the grace to keep going. Let's be those who run, with our eyes fixed on God and the good he has ahead, because we know our little is not a limitation in the limitless hands of our God; because we are strengthened in his grace through the running mates he gives; because he supplies what is needed in order for us to do what he is calling us to do today. Let's be those who run, with our eyes fixed on God and the good he has ahead, because our hearts are set on him, his praise and purposes, and our eternal home. Let's cross the finish line of this life, sprinting full on into eternity, for his glory. Let's be those whose lives show we have done what Jesus has said: remember Lot's wife!

ACKNOWLEDGMENTS

I am so grateful for the incredible team that helped get this book into your hands. I truly believe we are better together, and this book is a testimony to that.

To my husband, Nick: No one loves, supports, encourages, or believes in me like you do. Your love for Jesus, our family, and his purpose for our lives is the glue that holds this whole thing together. I love you with all my heart.

To my girls, Catherine and Sophia: Being your mum is the greatest joy of my life. Your brutal honesty keeps it real. Your humor keeps it fun. Your questions make me think. There's nothing like watching you grow and flourish as you pursue God's purpose for your own lives. I love you both so much.

To Elizabeth Prestwood: I am so grateful to have you alongside me as my collaborative writer. After working on so many books together, we have found our rhythm and flow, which makes the hard work of writing a book a great joy. I wouldn't want to do this without you and am so thankful to and for you.

To Rebekah Layton: This book wouldn't be what it is

without you. Thank you for reviewing every chapter. Your insight and contributions made all the difference, and your enthusiasm and commitment to this project helped to keep me going when I didn't think I could. You are a gift.

To Lysa TerKeurst: Thank you for walking through the initial phases of this book with me. And thank you for all the ideas you and your COMPEL team contributed to help make this book better. Your ideas, perspectives, inspiration, and suggestions were invaluable. I can never thank you enough for the friendship we share. I love you dearly.

To Julia, Slava, Liliia, Yuliia, Nadiia, Mi Yung, Andreas, Tony, Rhiannon, Barbara, Laura, Martin, Darren, Szymon, Kinga, Kamil, Ania, Dawn, and Angie: Thank you for the privilege of letting me include your stories. You inspire us all.

To the team at Thomas Nelson: Tim Paulson, Janet Talbert, Andrew Stoddard, Brigitta Nortker, Kristen Golden, Brian Scharp, Lisa Beech, Claire Drake, Sarah Van Cleve, Meg Schmidt, Mallory Collins, Stacey Altemari, Madeleine Kyger, *and everyone in sales.* Thank you for making yet another book come to life. Each of you poured your heart and soul into this project with great passion. *Janet,* you are such an encouraging editor. Your enthusiasm inspired me.

To Matt Yates: Thank you for believing in the message of this book and encouraging me through every phase of production. Your wisdom and years of experience are invaluable. You are such a gift to Nick and me. Thank you for being in our world.

To our A21, Propel, Zoe Church, and Equip & Empower teams, volunteers, partners, and supporters: Serving Jesus alongside you is the greatest privilege and honor of my life. Thank you for always being so open to share your stories. Let's keep changing the world together. I love you all so very much. A special thank you to *Katie Strandlund-Francois*, who always works tirelessly alongside me to ensure all the pieces of every book come together.

To my Lord and Savior, Jesus Christ: You are the reason I can never forget Lot's wife, the reason I can never look back, the reason I will keep moving forward until I'm home.

NOTES

INTRODUCTION
1. Genesis 19:26.
2. John 12:26.
3. Deuteronomy 31:8.
4. Hebrews 13:5.
5. Hebrews 12:2.
6. John 16:33.

CHAPTER 1: THE WORLD IS ALWAYS CHANGING, GOD REMAINS THE SAME
1. "Greek Immigration to Australia," Diaspora Travel Greece, accessed November 20, 2022, https://diasporatravelgreece. com/a-timeline-of-greek-immigration-to-australia/; Nikki Henningham, "Greece Born Community of Australia," Australian Women's Register, last modified November 20, 2018, https://www.womenaustralia.info/biogs/AWE2134b.htm.
2. Exodus 13:21.
3. Asha C. Gilbert, "Reports: Ukraine Bans All Male Citizens Ages 18 to 60 from Leaving the Country," *USA Today*, February 25, 2022, https://www.usatoday.com/story/news/world/2022 /02/25/russia-invasion-ukraine-bans-male-citizens-leaving /6936471001/.

4. Kaia Hubbard, "Here Are 10 of the Deadliest Natural Disasters in 2020," *U.S. News & World Report*, December 22, 2020, https://www.usnews.com/news/best-countries/slideshows/here-are-10-of-the-deadliest-natural-disasters-in-2020?slide=12.

5. Michelle Stoddart, "Cicada Invasion: After 17 Years Underground, Billions to Emerge This Spring," ABC News, April 10, 2021, https://abcnews.go.com/Politics/cicada-invasion-17-years-underground-billions-emerge-spring/story?id=76921532.

6. Frank Jordans and Pan Pylas, "Detentions, Injuries at Anti-Racism Protests Across Europe in Solidarity with US," Times of Israel, June 7, 2020, https://www.timesofisrael.com/detentions-injuries-at-anti-racism-protests-across-europe-in-solidarity-with-us; Savannah Smith, Jiachuan Wu, and Joe Murphy, "Map: George Floyd Protests Around the World," NBC News, June 9, 2020, https://www.nbcnews.com/news/world/map-george-floyd-protests-countries-worldwide-n1228391.

7. Hebrews 13:8.

8. Genesis 19:26.

9. Luke 17:32.

10. Jeremy Thompson, ed., *Lists of Biblical People, Places, Things, and Events* (Bellingham, WA: Faithlife, 2020).

11. Matthew 26:13.

12. Genesis 19:26 AMP.

13. *Merriam-Webster*, s.v. "longing (n.)," accessed January 19, 2023, https://www.merriam-webster.com/dictionary/longing.

14. Genesis 13:6.

15. Lauren Martin, "The Science Behind Nostalgia and Why We're So Obsessed with the Past," Elite Daily, July 17, 2014, https://www.elitedaily.com/life/science-behind-nostalgia-love-much/673184.

16. Martin, "Science Behind Nostalgia."

17. Stephanie Butler, "Off the Spice Rack: The History of Salt," History.com, updated August 22, 2018, https://www.history .com/news/off-the-spice-rack-the-story-of-salt.
18. Matthew 5:13.
19. *Merriam-Webster*, s.v. "linger (*v.*)," accessed January 19, 2023, https://www.merriam-webster.com/dictionary/linger.

CHAPTER 2: PREPARE YOUR HEART TO GO

1. Ecclesiastes 3:1–8, emphasis added.
2. Joshua 1:1–2.
3. Numbers 20:29.
4. 2 Samuel 11:26–27.
5. Genesis 50:3.
6. Deuteronomy 21:13; 1 Samuel 31:13.
7. Isaiah 61:3.
8. Genesis 37:34–35.
9. 1 Samuel 16:1.
10. Jeremiah 29:11.
11. Revelation 21:4.
12. Psalm 34:18.
13. Psalm 73:26.

CHAPTER 3: GO KNOWING WE ARE WHO HE SAYS WE ARE

1. "Case Study: Human Dignity and Forced Adoption in Australia," Australian Catholic University, 2014, https:// leocontent.acu.edu.au/file/95ea2ae3–7e9d-48e2-b904 -6e1bc5494663/16/Case_Study_Forced_Adoptions.pdf; Amber Jamieson, "Stories from the Mothers Who Had Their Babies Taken Away," Crikey, March 1, 2012, https://www .crikey.com.au/2012/03/01/forced-adoption-stories-from-the -mothers-who-had-their-babies-taken-away/.

2. Emily Ackew, "Brené Brown Explains the Misconception Around Feelings of Guilt and Shame," ABC News, December 1, 2021, https://www.abc.net.au/news/2021-12-02/brene-brown-ted -talk-emotions-shame-guilt-misconceptions-covid19/100669362.

3. "Illegitimacy," The Adoption History Project, accessed November 21, 2022, https://pages.uoregon.edu/adoption /topics/illegitimacy.htm.

4. Katherine Fenech, "Tears and Cheers as WA Apologises to Unwed Mums," WA Today, October 20, 2010, https://www .watoday.com.au/national/western-australia/tears-and-cheers -as-wa-apologises-to-unwed-mums-20101019–16sf8.html; "We're Sorry: South Australia to Apologise for Forced Adoption," *Newcastle Herald*; Katy Gallagher, "Forced Adoption—Apology," Legislative Assembly of the Australian Capital Territory: 3067–77, August 14, 2012; "Hundreds to Turn Out for Forced Adoptions Apology in NSW," News.com.au, September 20, 2012; "Apology for Forced Adoption Practices," Parliament of New South Wales, September 20, 2012; "Baillieu Apologises for Forced Adoption," *Sky News*, October 26, 2012; "Tas to Apologise over Forced Adoptions," Australian Broadcasting Corporation, August 6, 2012; "Queensland Government to Apologise for Past Forced Adoptions," press release, Government of Queensland, August 23, 2012.

5. Natalie Lynn, "20 Glorious Scriptures About God's Love," Bible Verses for You, January 6, 2022, https://bibleversesforyou .com/scriptures-about-gods-love/#:~:text=How%20Many%20 Times%20Does%20God,New%20Testament%20in%20the%20 KJV.

6. 1 John 3:1.

7. 1 John 1:5.

8. Numbers 23:19; Titus 1:2; Hebrews 6:18.

9. John 3:16.

10. Galatians 4:4–7.
11. 1 Corinthians 9:24–27; Hebrews 12:1.
12. 1 Peter 5:8.
13. Psalm 34:18.
14. Genesis 39.
15. Genesis 50:20.
16. Exodus 3:7–8.
17. Inspired by Dr. Joel Muddamalle's Instagram (@muddamalle) post, May 16, 2022.

CHAPTER 4: GO TO GROW

1. "The Great Hall," University of Sydney, https://www.sydney .edu.au/engage/visit/places-of-interest/great-hall.html.
2. Robert B. Sloan Jr., "Disciple," in *Holman Illustrated Bible Dictionary*, ed. Chad Brand et al. (Nashville, TN: Holman Bible Publishers, 2003), 425; *Merriam-Webster*, s.v. "disciple (*n.*)," accessed January 19, 2023, https://www.merriam-webster .com/dictionary/disciple.
3. Matthew 28:19–20.
4. "Growth Mindset," *Psychology Today*, accessed November 21, 2022, https://www.psychologytoday.com/us/basics/growth -mindset.
5. "5 Scriptures to Cultivate a Spiritual Growth Mindset," Robin Revis Pyke, April 28, 2022, https://robinrevispyke.com/2021 /04/28/5-scriptures-to-cultivate-a-spiritual-growth-mindset/.
6. "5 Scriptures"; *Merriam-Webster*, s.v. "mindset (*n.*)," accessed January 19, 2023, https://www.merriam-webster.com/dictionary /mindset.
7. "5 Scriptures."
8. "5 Scriptures."
9. "5 Scriptures."
10. Galatians 5:22–23.

11. Philippians 3:12–14.
12. 2 Timothy 4:7.
13. Psalm 92:12–15, emphasis added.
14. Giovanna Distefano and Bret H. Goodpaster, "Effects of Exercise and Aging on Skeletal Muscle," *Cold Spring Harbor Perspectives in Medicine* 8, no. 3 (March 2018): a029785, https://doi.org/10.1101%2Fcshperspect.a029785.
15. Oliver Page, "How to Leave Your Comfort Zone and Enter Your 'Growth Zone,'" Positive Psychology, November 4, 2020, https://positivepsychology.com/comfort-zone/.
16. John 15:16.
17. Romans 12:2.

CHAPTER 5: TAKE THE RISK AND GO AGAIN

1. 1 Kings 18:1–2.
2. 1 Kings 18:41–42.
3. 1 Kings 18:43.
4. 1 Kings 18:43–44.
5. 2 Corinthians 5:7.
6. 2 Timothy 1:7.
7. 1 Timothy 6:12.
8. *Merriam-Webster*, s.v. "again (*adv.*)," accessed January 20, 2023, https://www.merriam-webster.com/dictionary/again; Google's English Dictionary by Oxford Languages, s.v. "again (*adv.*)," https://www.google.com/search?q=again&rlz=1C5CHFA_enUS819US819&oq=again&aqs=chrome.0.69i59j69i57l2j69i60l5.857j0j7&sourceid=chrome&ie=UTF-8.
9. 1 Kings 18:41.
10. Hebrews 11:1.
11. Romans 4:17–18.
12. 2 Timothy 4:7.
13. Matthew 25:23.

CHAPTER 6: GO WITH WHAT YOU HAVE

1. Luke 9:62.
2. 1 Samuel 14:6.
3. Exodus 4:1–3.
4. Joshua 2:15–17.
5. 1 Samuel 17:40.
6. 2 Kings 4:1–7.
7. Matthew 10:42.
8. Mark 6:20–52.
9. John 6:1–13.
10. Zechariah 4:10 NLT.
11. 2 Corinthians 2:11.
12. 1 Kings 17:12–14.
13. Mark 12:43–44.
14. *Merriam-Webster*, s.v. "procrastinate (*v.*)," emphasis added, accessed January 20, 2023, https://www.merriam-webster.com/dictionary/procrastinate.
15. 1 Kings 17:15–16.
16. Luke 17:6.
17. Luke 16:10.
18. 1 Kings 17:13 NIV.
19. 1 Corinthians 3:6–8.

CHAPTER 7: DON'T GO IT ALONE

1. Ecclesiastes 4:9–10.
2. Galatians 6:2.
3. Romans 12:13.
4. 1 Thessalonians 5:14.
5. Romans 12:15; "You Can't Do Life Alone," Northstar Church, December 3, 2015, https://northstar.church/you-cant-do-life-alone/; Christina Fox, "Don't Go It Alone, God Made Us for Community," Christianity.com, August 8, 2022, https://www

.christianity.com/wiki/christian-life/don-t-go-it-alone-you
-were-made-for-community.html.

6. Exodus 17:11–13.

7. Ruth 1:16–17.

8. Ruth 4:16–17.

9. 1 Samuel 18:1.

10. 1 Samuel 20:41.

11. Steve Walton, "Corinth in Acts: Paul's Financial Support,"
Bible Odyssey, accessed November 22, 2022, https://www
.bibleodyssey.org/places/related-articles/corinth-in-acts
-pauls-financial-support/.

12. "Paul's Ministry Team," Canadian Bible Guy, accessed
November 22, 2022, https://canadianbibleguy.com/2017/09/18
/pauls-ministry-team/.

13. "Paul and His Collaborators," International Seminar on Saint
Paul, April 19–29, 2009, https://www.paulus.net/sisp/doc
/Wawa_eng.pdf; "The Companions of Paul & Biblical Persons
Related to Paul," Christian Pilgrimage Journeys, accessed
November 22, 2022, https://www.christian-pilgrimage
-journeys.com/biblical-sources/apostle-paul-life-teaching
-theology/companions-of-paul/; Romans 16:1–16.

14. Philippians 2:19–22; Kelli Mahoney, "Examples of Friendship
in the Bible," Learn Religions, June 25, 2019, https://www
.learnreligions.com/examples-of-friendship-in-the-bible
-712377; "Paul and Timothy," Fuller Theological Seminary,
accessed November 22, 2022, https://www.fuller.edu/next
-faithful-step/resources/paul-and-timothy/.

15. Mark 6:7; Luke 10:1.

16. Matthew 17:1; "Why Did Jesus Choose Peter, James, and John
to Be His Inner Circle?," Got Questions, accessed November 22,
2022, https://www.gotquestions.org/Jesus-inner-circle.html.

17. John 13:23; 21:7.

18. John 19:26.
19. Luke 8:1–3.
20. Luke 8:1–3; Matthew 27:55–56.
21. Luke 10.
22. John 12:1–3; Aubrey Coleman, "How Jesus Modeled True Friendship," *Daily Grace* (blog), accessed November 22, 2022, https://thedailygraceco.com/blogs/the-daily-grace-blog/how -jesus-modeled-true-friendship.
23. John 11:3.
24. John 11:21, 32; Mahoney, "Examples of Friendship in the Bible."
25. Mahoney, "Examples of Friendship in the Bible."
26. John 15:13–16.
27. John 15:5.
28. Ephesians 4:15; Rachel Prochnow, "10 Qualities of Godly Friend," Rachel Prochnow, January 22, 2020, https://rachel prochnow.com/10-qualities-of-godly-friend/.
29. Proverbs 17:17.
30. Proverbs 27:17.
31. Hebrews 10:24–25.
32. Mark 2:3–5, 11–12.
33. Jennie Allen, *Find Your People: Building Deep Community in a Lonely World*, 1st ed. (Colorado Springs: WaterBrook, 2022), 23.
34. Allen, *Find Your People*.
35. Genesis 1:27.
36. Allen, *Find Your People*.

CHAPTER 8: ARISE AND GO: THINGS CHANGE WHEN WE DO

1. Judges 5:7 NIV.
2. Bible Sense Lexicon / Holman Concordance.
3. *Merriam-Webster*, s.v. "arise (*v.*)," accessed January 20, 2023, https://www.merriam-webster.com/dictionary/arise.

4. *Merriam-Webster*, s.v. "posture (*n*.)," accessed January 20, 2023, https://www.merriam-webster.com/dictionary/posture.

5. *Merriam-Webster*, s.v. "slouch (*n*.)," accessed January 20, 2023, https://www.merriam-webster.com/dictionary/slouch.

6. Ephesians 6:12.

7. Ephesians 6:11–13.

8. 1 Timothy 6:12.

9. Hebrews 12:1–2.

10. Ephesians 5:14.

11. Ephesians 6:13.

12. 1 Corinthians 6:19.

13. Romans 12:2.

14. Philippians 4:8.

15. "Ezekiel 16:49," Bible Study Tools, https://www.biblestudytools.com/commentaries/gills-exposition-of-the-bible/ezekiel-16-49.html.

16. Ezekiel 16:49–50 NIV.

17. 2 Corinthians 1:3–6.

18. Exodus 3.

19. Joshua 1:2.

20. Judges 6.

21. 1 Samuel 16:12.

22. 1 Kings 17:9.

23. Jeremiah 18:1.

24. Esther 4.

25. Nehemiah 2.

26. Mark 5:41.

27. Luke 7:14 AMP.

28. Mark 3:3 AMP.

29. John 5:8.

30. John 5:17.

31. Romans 6:10–11.

32. Ephesians 2:10.

CONCLUSION

1. Hebrews 13:14 NLT.
2. 1 Peter 2:11–12 ESV.
3. John R. Spencer, "Sojourner," in *The Anchor Yale Bible Dictionary*, ed. David Noel Freedman (New York: Doubleday, 1992), 103.
4. Hebrews 11:8–9 BLB.
5. "Visit the U.S.," U.S. Citizenship and Immigration Services, accessed November 22, 2022, https://www.uscis.gov/visit-the-us.
6. "Visit the U.S."
7. "What Are the Benefits and Responsibilities of Citizenship?," USCIS.gov, accessed November 22, 2022, https://www.uscis .gov/sites/default/files/document/guides/chapter2.pdf.
8. Philippians 3:20–21 GNT.
9. Joshua 13.
10. John 6:38.
11. John 5:19; 12:49; 14:31.
12. Strong's Concordance, s.v. "telos (*n.*)," accessed January 20, 2023, https://biblehub.com/greek/5056.htm; See also s.v. "teleios (*adj.*)," https://biblehub.com/greek/5046.htm and s.v. "teleioó (*v.*)," https://biblehub.com/greek/5048.htm.
13. Acts 13:36.
14. "Telos: Orienting Ourselves to God's Ultimate Purpose," *The High Calling* (blog), accessed November 22, 2022, https:// www.theologyofwork.org/the-high-calling/blog/telos -orienting-ourselves-gods-ultimate-purpose.
15. Acts 20:24.
16. 2 Corinthians 5:20.
17. "What Are the Roles of a Diplomat?," National Museum of American Diplomacy, October 11, 2022, https://diplomacy.state .gov/diplomacy/what-are-the-roles-of-a-diplomat/.

18. Acts 11:26.
19. 1 Corinthians 15:55–56.
20. Psalm 113:4–6; 139:7–10.
21. Daniel 8:16; Luke 1:26–38; Revelation 12:7–12.
22. Ezekiel 1:1–28.
23. Isaiah 65:21–22.
24. Hebrews 12:1.
25. Revelation 21:4.
26. Revelation 7:15–17.
27. Philippians 3:21.
28. This list and ideas inspired by the following article: Russell Gehrlein, "What Will Work Be like in the New Heaven and Earth?," Institute for Faith, Work, and Economics, October 12, 2017, https://tifwe.org/what-will-work-be-like-in-the-new-heaven-and-earth/.
29. Revelation 21:3.
30. Revelation 7:9–10.
31. Revelation 22:5.
32. 1 John 2:17 NIV.
33. John 14:2–3.
34. Revelation 22:1–3.
35. Revelation 7:15–17.
36. Revelation 21:18–21.
37. Hebrews 11:40.
38. 1 Corinthians 9:24.
39. Romans 6:10–11.
40. Numbers 23:19; Hebrews 13:8; James 1:17.
41. Psalm 33:4; 1 Corinthians 1:19.
42. 1 John 4:4.
43. 1 John 1:5.
44. Matthew 19:26; Mark 10:27.
45. Deuteronomy 4:31; 31:8; Hebrews 4:16.

46. 2 Corinthians 12:9–10.
47. John 15:8.
48. Acts 20:24.

ABOUT THE AUTHOR

Christine Caine is a speaker, activist, and bestselling author. She and her husband, Nick, founded the A21 Campaign, an anti–human trafficking organization. They also founded Propel Women, an initiative that is dedicated to coming alongside women all over the globe to activate their God-given purpose. You can tune into Christine's weekly podcast, *Equip & Empower*, or her TBN television program to be encouraged with the hope of Jesus wherever you are. To learn more about Christine, visit www.christinecaine.com.